MODERN FREIGHT CARS

ROLLING STOCK FROM THE '60s THROUGH TODAY

Jeff Wilson

Kalmbach
Media

On the cover: On June 26, 2005, a former Burlington Northern SD60M and Santa Fe GP60M thread a manifest freight between a variety of freight cars in BNSF Railway's Galesburg, Ill., classification yard. Tom Danneman photo.
Contents page: An aerial view shows the bowl portion of Union Pacific's West Colton Yard in Colton, Calif., in April 2014. Brian Schmidt photo.

Kalmbach Media
21027 Crossroads Circle
Waukesha, Wisconsin 53186
www.KalmbachHobbyStore.com

Published in 2019
26 25 24 23 22   2 3 4 5 6

Manufactured in China

ISBN: 978-1-62700-585-2
EISBN: 978-1-62700-586-9

Editor: Eric White
Book Design: Lisa Bergman

Library of Congress Control Number: 2018941172

Contents

Introduction

So what constitutes a "modern" freight car? For the purposes of this book we're starting the timeline in 1960. Why 1960? For starters, that's where my earlier book, *Freight Cars of the '40s and '50s*, left off, so this book provides a natural continuation.

A better reason, however, is that although 1960 was more than 50 years ago, it was a pivotal point in freight car evolution. 1960 marks a time when cars were becoming longer and heavier. Cars with 70-ton capacity were replacing older 50-ton cars, with 100-ton cars on the horizon. Roller-bearing trucks were appearing in increasing numbers.

Changes in shipping rates were leading to development of specialized freight cars, meaning the general-service boxcar was no longer expected to carry everything. The 1960s saw the introduction or growth of jumbo covered hoppers for grain service, large bathtub coal gondolas, 86- and 60-foot auto-parts boxcars, 89-foot multi-level auto racks, 89-foot piggyback flatcars, center-beam lumber cars, and coil-steel flatcars. Tank cars were transitioning to frameless designs, larger tanks, and specialized fittings.

Car size and weight has continued to grow in the past few years, with a move toward 110-ton cars. The number of specialty cars continues to grow, while the boxcar fleet continues to shrink.

Although freight cars built in 1960 are out of service, some from the later part of the decade have been rebuilt and remain in service in the late 2010s. Car rules, which once mandated a 40-year lifespan for cars, now allow 50 years with rebuilding (more on that in Chapter 1), meaning that today you can find a mix of new cars as well as many upgraded cars from the 1970s and 1980s.

And some cars have disappeared. The 40-foot boxcar was fading away by the 1960s, as were stock cars and ice-bunker refrigerator cars (neither of which are included in this book).

What you'll find

The first chapter looks at how cars evolved from the 1960s through today, with a look at specific manufacturers, size and weight restrictions, and car-use rules and regulations that affect car design and operations. As modelers, this information will help you put together a realistic car fleet based on the period, railroad, and region you model.

Subsequent chapters look at specific car types, with guidelines on design, specific lading requirements, and number of cars in service. Car ownership is explained, with a look at private- vs. railroad-owned cars, the burst of shortline-owned per-diem boxcars in the late 1970s, and freight car pools such as Trailer Train flatcars and intermodal cars, Railbox boxcars, and Railgon gondolas.

Chapter 10 looks at specific components found on all types of cars, including wheels, trucks, couplers, cushion underframes, and brake components, again showing how they work and how they're used.

This book is not meant to be a complete guide to every modern freight car built. It includes information on basic spotting features and details and basic car identification, but the sheer number of cars (and variations) precludes going into excessive detail or roster information on each variation.

Indeed, there are a number of outstanding books on the market that cover specific car models. If you're looking for more in-depth information on specific cars, the bibliography on page 110 provides a good starting point.

Turn the page and we'll get started with an overview of freight cars, including car design, evolution, and manufacturers.

Acknowledgements

Thanks to the many individuals who provided photographs and information for this book, especially Tom Danneman, Cody Grivno, J. David Ingles, James Kinkaid, and Keith Kohlmann. Thanks also to the many modelers, rail enthusiasts, and historians who have authored books and articles with detailed information, statistics, and photo guides of freight cars. Their work proved invaluable in putting this book together.

Several new aluminum BethGon coal gondolas stand out in this Union Pacific train rolling across Nebraska in 2006. *Jeff Wilson*

1

CHAPTER ONE

Freight car evolution and design

The North American freight car fleet has changed dramatically since the early 1960s. The traditional general-purpose boxcar is largely gone, replaced by an ever-increasing number of specialized freight car types, **1**. There's been growth in freight car weight limits and car size. Meanwhile, the number of car manufacturers has dropped significantly, with remaining builders producing cars on a large scale.

Most modern freight cars are specialized, designed to carry a specific lading, and unit trains (like this train of ethanol tank cars) have become common. *Jeff Wilson*

2 The 1960s and later saw a rise in "jumbo" cars as weight limits increased and railroads gained favorable rates on them. This ACF 5,250-cf capacity Center Flow covered hopper has four bays with pneumatic outlets. It was built in 1980. *R.J. Wilhelm; J. David Ingles collection*

3 Adding the load limit and light weight shows this is a 220,000-pound GRL (70-ton) car. Other lettering includes the reporting marks, number, plate clearance, the AAR designation of XF (restricted to food service), and that the car was weighed when built in 1978. *R.J. Wilhelm; J. David Ingles collection*

Freight car age

Railcars last a long time, so those currently in service (early 2019 as of this writing) are for the most part cars built in the 1970s and later. The length of time a car can remain in service, including rebuilding, is regulated by the Federal Railroad Administration (FRA) and Association of American Railroads (AAR).

Cars built since July 1974 can be operated in interchange service for 50 years, and since 2005 that can be extended another 15 years (called Increased Life Status) with testing and rebuilding (under AAR Rule 88).

Cars built prior to July 1974 can run in interchange service for 40 years (AAR Rule 90), which can be extended for another 10 years with rebuilding (including specified required upgrades).

Note that these rules apply to cars in interchange service. Cars used strictly on line, or those converted to work or maintenance-of-way (MOW) service, can be older.

The FRA is the federal agency responsible for overseeing regulations and operating rules. An agency of the U.S. Department of Transportation (DOT), the FRA was created in 1966. The AAR, founded in 1934, is a rail industry trade association that issues and publishes service rules and interchange rules, compiles industry data, and establishes industry standards.

In addition, the AAR has two subsidiaries: Railinc, which provides information technology services, and the Transportation Technology Center Inc. (TTCI), which operates a test railroad at Pueblo, Colo., and is responsible for testing new equipment and technology.

Car capacity and size

Freight car size had been increasing throughout the early diesel era, but the 1960s saw a dramatic increase in "jumbo" cars of various types to take advantage of new rules on rates, **2**. Car size is rated by—and regulated according to—both overall dimensions and weight.

In terms of capacity, cars are known by their nominal carrying capacity in tons: 110-ton, 100-ton, and 70-ton (up from the 40- and 50-ton cars most common during the steam and early diesel eras). This is important both in terms of how much cargo can be loaded in a car, and in what routes can handle cars of various weights.

However, although these descriptions are commonly used, they are just rough estimates of a car's load limit. The actual capacity of any given car varies by the car's unloaded (light) weight. The key number is the Gross Rail Load, or GRL. This is the total weight allowed on the rails for a car, and is calculated by adding a car's light weight plus the weight of the load.

Look at the stenciling on any freight car and you'll see the light weight and load limit in pounds, rounded to the nearest 100 (there used to be a line for "capacity" but it was an estimation—it was eliminated in 1989), **3**. Adding the light weight and load limit gives you the GRL.

Over the years the AAR has set GRL limits for unrestricted interchange along with higher limits for restricted interchange.

Into the early 1960s, 50-ton cars (then a GRL of 169,000 pounds) were the standard for unrestricted interchange anywhere on the rail system. There were also plenty of 70-ton (210,000-pound GRL) and 100-ton (251,000-pound GRL) cars in service, but they were allowed only on certain routes.

Railroads wanted the increased capacity of larger cars, and provided for this by improving track and using heavier rail—first on main routes, then on secondary lines and, in some cases, branch lines. In 1963 the AAR increased the weight limits for each weight class: to 263,000 pounds for 100-ton cars, 220,000 for 70-ton cars, and 177,000 for 50-ton cars. This marked the true start of the 100-ton car as standard, although many 70-ton cars would continue to be built.

Effective in January 1995, the AAR approved the use of 110-ton cars with a GRL of 286,000 pounds (AAR standard S-259, issued in November 1994), including specifications for car and truck/journal design to handle the increased weight. Some railroads had

Former car manufacturers

Many companies have built freight cars in the modern era. This is a summary of car manufacturers that were building cars in 1960 or later but have since gone out of business or been acquired by or merged into other companies.

Berwick Freight Car Co.: Began as Berwick Foundry & Forge, acquiring ACF's former Berwick, Pa., plant after it closed in 1961. BF&F closed in 1982 and shortly reopened as Berwick Freight Car, building cars until 1993.

Bethlehem Steel Car Co.: Bethlehem Steel Corp.'s freight car division was formed in 1923 with the purchase of Midvale Steel and Ordnance. The division built freight cars until it was sold to Johnstown America in 1991; that company was renamed FreightCar America in 2004.

CNCF: Mexican builder Constructora Nacional de Carros de Ferrocarril built boxcars for IPD owners as well as Mexican railroads from 1979 through the early 1980s.

Evans Products Co.: A long-time builder of car components, Evans bought U.S. Railway Equipment Co. in the 1960s and operated it as a leasing company. The company built cars (mainly coil steel cars, covered hoppers, and boxcars) under the Evans name. Evans also acquired SIECO in the 1970s. Evans ceased building cars in 1984.

FMC Corporation: Built freight cars from 1965-1985 at Springfield, Ore.; the plant was purchased by Gunderson in 1985.

General American Car Co.: A major builder of cars through most of the 1900s, the company began as the German-American Car Co., but changed its name in 1916. General American had multiple divisions and also operated a leasing company. It ceased building cars in 1984, and its designs were licensed to Trinity. Successor GATX Corp. still operates as a car leasing company.

Greenville Steel Car Co.: Began as Greenville (Pa.) Metal Products Co. in 1910; acquired its name in 1914 and built new cars from 1916 into the 1980s. It was acquired by Trinity in 1986.

Gulf Railcar: Built tank cars at the former Richmond Tank Car plant from 1983 into the 1990s.

Hawker Siddeley Canada (later listed as Hawker Siddeley Canada Ltd., Trenton Works Division): Built cars in Trenton, Nova Scotia from 1962 until 1988. Best known for building Canadian cylindrical covered hoppers. Plant was eventually sold to Greenbrier.

Ingalls Shipbuilding: Built cars in 1979 and 1980 for North American Car Co.

Magor Car Corp.: Built freight cars beginning in the 1910s. It became a division of Fruehauf in 1964 and ceased building freight cars in 1973.

Marine Industries Ltd.: Canadian company based in Sorel-Tracy, Quebec. Built railcars from 1957 to 1986, notably Canadian cylindrical covered hoppers and also flats and gondolas.

North American Car Co.: Built cars and also operated as a leasing company. Its designs were sold to Trinity and Thrall in 1985.

Ortner Freight Car Co.: Primarily a builder of hopper cars; it was acquired by Trinity in 1984.

Pacific Car & Foundry: Incorporated as Seattle Car & Foundry in 1911, merged with another builder and became PC&F in 1917. It became a subsidiary of AC&F in 1924, and specialized in refrigerator cars. Its parent company became Paccar in 1972; it ceased railcar manufacturing shortly after 1980.

Portec: Known mainly for building auto racks (acquiring Paragon in the early 1970s), the company also built freight cars and components from the late 1970s into the 1980s.

Pullman-Standard: One of the country's largest car builders through the 1970s. It was formed by a merger of Pullman Co.'s freight car division and Standard Steel Car in 1930. Its designs and several plants were acquired by Trinity in 1984.

Richmond Tank Car Co.: Built tank cars and also covered hoppers from the 1940s to 1983; plant located in Houston, Texas. Gulf Railcar later took over the plant and built tank cars into the 1990s.

Southern Iron & Equipment Co. (SIECO): A long-time rebuilder of steam locomotives and other equipment, the company built freight cars and was best known for its 50-foot per-diem boxcars starting in 1973; it was acquired by Evans in the 1970s.

Thrall Car Manufacturing Co.: Formed in 1917 in Chicago, it had become the country's no. 2 car builder when acquired by Trinity in 2001. Produced most car types except tanks. Acquired auto rack builders Whitehead & Kales and Portec (Paragon) in the 1980s.

Trenton Works: See Hawker Siddeley.

U.S. Railway Equipment Co.: A Chicago company (later a division of Evans) that mainly rebuilt cars, but built some new cars, from the 1950s to 1978.

been using such cars since 1991 under bilateral agreements, based on track and bridge strengths on specific routes. They use can still be limited on some routes.

Many in the industry see the coming of even heavier cars, with a GRL of 315,000 pounds (125-ton cars). Railroads have been upgrading main routes to handle such cars, but widespread approval is still in the future. These cars require 7" x 12" journals and 38" wheels (compared to 6½" x 12" journals and 36" wheels for 286K cars). Some railcar manufacturers are offering cars that can be converted (to fit the new, larger trucks).

It's important to note that many cars still fall well under the maximum GRLs, depending upon the products they carry. Unit-train coal gondolas, for example, are designed to carry as much coal by weight as possible, and will almost always max out their load limits.

On the other hand, many of the huge 86-foot, high-cube auto parts boxcars built in the 1960s and '70s

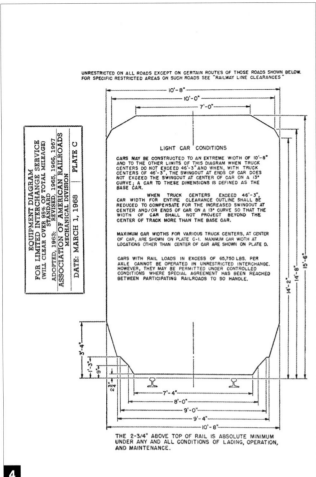

4

Plate diagrams (this is Plate C) show car height and width limits. Published by the AAR, they are revised periodically. *AAR*

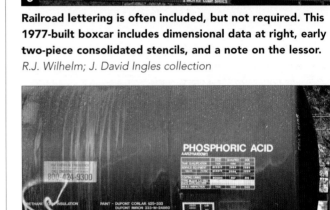

5

Railroad lettering is often included, but not required. This 1977-built boxcar includes dimensional data at right, early two-piece consolidated stencils, and a note on the lessor. *R.J. Wilhelm; J. David Ingles collection*

6

Lettering on this tank car includes the AAR tank designation, testing-data matrix, and hazmat placard and lettering for phosphoric acid. It has the modern three-panel consolidated stencil. *Jeff Wilson*

were 70-ton cars. The metal stampings these cars carried were bulky but not heavy, and a load that completely filled the car interior might only weigh about 20 tons. The higher weight limit was not needed.

This is why the various GRL limits are in place: It's still more cost-effective to build a lower-capacity car, because the components required will be lighter and less expensive. In the 2010s, 80 percent of cars added to the fleet have been 286K (110-ton) cars.

Many 263K cars have been upgraded to 286K as well. For most of these, it was a matter of upgrading the truck capacity, as the carbodies had been built to handle the higher weight.

Plate designations

Along with weight, railcar size (exterior height and width) is also regulated to make sure cars will fit under bridges, pass through tunnels, and safely pass on parallel tracks, loading docks, and other tight clearance areas.

"Plate" diagrams, indicated by letters, were developed by the AAR to provide a guideline for rolling stock clearance. For each Plate designation, a diagram shows a car outline with maximum allowable dimensions at various car heights, **4**. For this and other Plate diagrams, instructions (and an additional diagram) call for reducing the width of long cars if the end or middle overhang on a curve becomes excessive.

Plate B clearance, first adopted in 1948, means a car is unrestricted for interchange and can travel on any route. The basic outside dimensions include an exterior height of 15'-1" (above railhead) and width of 10'-8" (the maximum for any Plate diagram).

Plate C clearance was adopted in 1963, and at the time provided clearance on 95 percent of routes. It allows a height of 15'-6". In 1974 came Plate E (15'-9") and Plate F (17'-0"), the latter for high-cube boxcars. Plate H (1994) was adopted for double-stack container cars, allowing a 20'-2" height. Specifically for enclosed auto racks are Plate J (2005), allowing a 19'-0" height, and Plate K (2005) which allows a 20'-3" height but narrows the width to 10'-0".

Since the early 1970s, freight cars larger than Plate B have a stencil on the side indicating its clearance, **3**. If a car's dimensions exceed a particular Plate designation, it is marked "exceeds Plate X." Plate diagrams are periodically reviewed and revised.

You can find these diagrams published in *Official Railway Equipment Registers*, along with other information on car restrictions and use.

Freight car timeline, post-1960

1960—First multi-level open auto rack cars placed in service
1963—Gross Rail Load (GRL) limits increased
1963—First 86-foot high-cube boxcars placed in service
1964—First jumbo wood chip gondolas placed in service
1964—First rotary-dump, unit-train coal gondolas enter service
1966—Roller-bearing trucks required on all new/rebuilt 100-ton cars
1966—Running boards no longer required on new cars
1967—ACI (Automatic Car Identification) labels begin appearing on cars
1968—Roller-bearing trucks required on all new freight cars
1970—Tank car size limited to 34,500 gallons
1970—Cast-iron ("chilled") wheels banned from interchange service
1970—ACI labels required on all cars
1971—Shelf-style couplers required on tank cars
1972—Consolidated stencils begin appearing
1974—The first Railbox boxcars enter service

1975—ARA tank cars no longer allowed in service
1977—First significant order of center-beam flatcars delivered
1977—ACI system abandoned
1978—Wheel-inspection dots appear on cars currently in service
1981—First double-stack container cars placed in service
1983—Running boards to be removed from all house cars (originally 1974)
1985—Capacity data lettering no longer required on new cars
1989—First all-purpose intermodal spine cars in service
1990—Cryogenic refrigerator cars enter service
1994—AEI tags required on all cars
1995—Solid-bearing trucks banned from interchange
1995—110-ton (286,000 GRL) cars approved for interchange
1999—53-foot well cars enter service
2003—TTX begins shortening 45- and 48-foot wells to 40 feet
2003—TBOX and FBOX boxcars begin appearing
2015—New tank car (DOT-117) specifications are released

Painting and lettering

Car painting and lettering—both general trends and specific requirements—have evolved over time. Through the steam/diesel transition era, various shades of oxide red (often called "boxcar red") dominated cars, especially boxcars, with black typical for hopper and tank cars and yellow and orange of many refrigerator cars.

The 1960s saw broader use of color, with more cars painted in the company colors of their owners. This continued with the bright per-diem boxcars and elevator-owned covered hoppers of the 1970s and continues on some cars through today.

Lettering includes elements that are both optional and required. Many railroads and private owners include a logo or herald along with spelled-out railroad or company name and other identifying lettering, **5**, but this isn't required. It does, however, serve as a type of free rolling billboard.

Perhaps the most important lettering are the required reporting marks and number, which are unique to each car. Reporting marks are a group of two to four letters, and are assigned to each railroad and private owner by the AAR. Privately owned cars' marks end in an "X."

The road number for each car is unique to that set of reporting marks. The reporting marks and number are placed on each side and end of each car as prescribed by regulations.

Weight and dimensional data are also required, **5**. In general, the weight information (load limit and light weight) are on the left of each side, with dimensional data (interior and exterior width and height, and often cubic capacity) on the right.

Tank cars include the Department of Transportation car code along with tank test dates and data, **6**. As Chapter 3 explains, this can also include hazmat placards and stenciling including lading.

Other lettering includes the type of wheels, couplers, brake pads, and other equipment, along with specific loading restrictions or instructions, as well as door (or valve or outlet gate) operating instructions. Manufacturer logos often appear as well.

The consolidated stencil, which began appearing in 1972, carries the car's built date and inspection and maintenance information, **5, 6**. This includes COTS (clean, oil, test, and stencil), IDT (in-date test for brake inspection), and LUB (lubrication date for roller bearings) or RPKD (for repacking journal boxes). All cars were to have these panels by 1979.

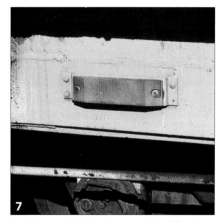

7

An Automatic Equipment Identification (AEI) tag is located along the side sill at the right end of each side. They became mandatory in 1994. *Jeff Wilson*

These have evolved from single or double (separate) panels to a combined double panel to today's three-panel design, with the a narrow bottom panel for built/rebuilt dates.

Cars assigned to a specific manufacturer or service have routing or loading stenciled on each side, such as "return to ___ when empty" or "for ____ loading only."

Since 1994, each freight car must carry an Automatic Equipment Identification (AEI) tag, **7**. This is a small box located on each side of a car that houses a radio transponder that responds to trackside readers to

The first attempt at electronic car tracking was Automatic Car Identification (ACI), which used colored stripes on a panel read by optical trackside scanners. *Jeff Wilson*

Number of cars in service by type		
	2010	**2017**
Boxcars	142,000	133,000
Covd Hpr	479,000	585,000
Tank	306,000	432,000
Flat	198,000	155,000
Intermodal	161,000	201,940
IM flats	77,000	73,122
Hopper	168,000	135,000
Gondola	241,000	231,000
Reefer	15,500	8,000
Total	1,596,000	1,632,000

Sources: AAR UMLER reports (revenue cars only), misc. AAR reports, *Official Railway Equipment Register*, various editions

communicate car identity and other information as cars roll by.

An earlier attempt at automated identification was ACI (Automatic Car Identification), introduced in 1967 and mandated for all interchange cars by 1970, **8**. This was an optical system that used trackside scanners to read bar-code plates (black plates with colored horizontal bands) on cars. The system didn't work well—grime made reading panels unreliable—and the system was abandoned in 1977. Many cars could still be found with old ACI plates into the 2000s.

Reflective strips have been required on new rolling stock since 2005, and all freight cars were to be equipped by 2015. Strips can be vertical or horizontal, and placement varies by car type, with a minimum of 3.5 square feet of reflective material on each side.

Manufacturers

Freight car manufacturing is currently dominated by six major builders: American Railcar Industries/ACF, FreightCar America, Greenbrier/Gunderson, National Steel Car, TrinityRail, and Union Tank Car. Several other companies have built significant numbers of cars since 1960 but are no longer in business—see "Former Car Manufacturers" on page 7. In addition, many railroads have built cars in their own shops.

Car building is a very cyclical business, depending heavily upon the economy, which drives traffic levels. Manufacturers often find themselves in a feast-or-famine situation, seemingly either producing cars as fast as they can or having a surplus of cars and production capacity with no orders.

This has led to larger companies acquiring small builders, with many smaller companies that specialized in certain car types going out of business, merging, or being bought out by larger companies.

Most car builders today have diversified into other related industries, or are owned by parent companies that manufacture other products. Most have also smoothed out production cycles by also owning their own fleets of cars for leasing and by supplying parts and providing repair and rebuilding services.

Here's a brief summary of the major car manufacturers active as of early 2019:

TrinityRail, a division of Trinity Industries, is the largest supplier of new cars as of 2018. It began as Trinity Steel in Dallas, Texas, in 1933. The company entered the rail business by building tank car bodies under contract to other builders in the late 1960s, then began building its own line of cars (initially tank cars and covered hoppers) in 1978.

Trinity has since bought, merged, or acquired the designs and/or manufacturing facilities of several other builders, including General American

(1984), Pullman-Standard (1984), Ortner (1984), Greenville (1986), and Thrall (2001). The company offers a full line of freight car types.

Greenbrier, the second-largest builder, began as a steel fabricating company owned by the Gunderson brothers in Portland, Ore., in 1919. The company began building freight car underframes under contract in 1958. The Springfield (Eugene), Ore., plant was owned by FMC Corporation from 1965 to 1985, and operated as the Marine and Rail Equipment Division of FMC. This plant was sold in 1985 to the Greenbrier Companies, which had been officially named such in 1981, and began building cars as Gunderson Inc. The Gunderson name became The Greenbrier Companies in 1994, and the company acquired Trenton Works in 1995. Greenbrier builds cars of most types at plants in Oregon, Mexico, and other countries.

American Railcar Industries (ARI) was formed in 1994 as a railcar-building subsidiary of ACF Industries. ACF (American Car & Foundry until 1955) had been one of the country's largest car manufacturers since 1899, when it was formed by the merger of 13 companies. ARI continues to build tank and covered hopper cars based on ACF designs at plants in Paragould and Marmaduke, Ark. ACF provides parts, components, tanks, and conversion and rebuilding services at its Milton, Pa., plant.

FreightCar America (FCA) traces its roots to the Bethlehem Steel Car Co., which began building cars in 1923. That company was acquired by Johnstown America in 1991. The company changed its name to FreightCar America in December 2004. FCA specializes in coal gondolas and hopper cars, but also builds covered hoppers, flatcars, and boxcars at assembly plants in Cherokee, Ala., and Roanoke, Va.

National Steel Car (NSC) is a Canadian company, based in Hamilton, Ontario. It began building freight cars in 1912 and has the largest single-site manufacturing facility in North America. The company built cars under license to Pullman-Standard through the 1970s and currently builds cars of all types for railroads and private owners in Canada, the United States, and Mexico.

Union Tank Car (UTLX) is best known for its leasing fleet of tank cars. The company began operating in the 1860s and had long designed cars—but did not build them—until acquiring Graver Tank Co. in 1955. Since then the company has manufactured cars for its own fleet and for sale and lease. It operates plants in Alexandria, Va., and Sheldon, Texas.

Car design/fleets

The major evolution in the freight car fleet in the past few decades has been the shift in preference toward various specialty car types. The ubiquitous 40-foot general-purpose boxcar was the most-common car type through the 1950s. Boxcars carried all manner of cased and crated goods, bulk products like grain, and many large, heavy items—including automobiles.

By the 1960s, specialty cars were on the increase: Short covered hoppers for cement and sand and large covered hoppers for grain and plastic pellets; 89-foot auto racks and piggyback flatcars; specialized tank cars for LPG, chlorine, anhydrous ammonia, and many other products; flatcars for coiled steel; jumbo gondolas for unit coal trains; and many others.

Many boxcars were still being built, but they were specialized as well. Examples were the 60- and 86-foot auto parts boxcars designed to carry racks of parts; plug-door insulated cars for canned goods, beverages, and food products; and all-door boxcars for lumber products.

Today, the covered hopper is the dominant car type, making up 26 percent of the total freight car fleet, followed by tank cars at 19 percent. Boxcars are just 7 percent of the total—and just 15 percent of those are general-purpose cars. See the chart on page 10 for a summary through the years.

In 2010, the average age of a freight car was just over 19 years, but boxcars are becoming old: The average age of a boxcar was 25, compared to 16 for a tank car. As of early 2018, the average age of a freight car was 19.5 years old.

In the 1960s, most freight cars were owned by the railroads themselves. Exceptions were tank cars (virtually all of which are owned by leasing companies or private owners), refrigerator cars, most of which were privately owned, and piggyback flats, where Trailer Train (TTX) dominated ownership.

Through the next few decades, private lease fleets began dominating covered hopper ownership. Intermodal equipment numbers grew tremendously, with most owned by TTX. And as unit coal trains expanded, many utilities chose to acquire their own car fleets.

In 1977, railroads owned 1.3 million freight cars, which was 80 percent of the total fleet. By 2015 this had dropped to 420,000 cars, or 29 percent.

The total number of cars in service has been dropping, but average car capacity has risen (from 79 tons to 105 tons between 1980 and the 2010s) and revenue ton-miles have also increased, meaning railroads are more efficient with cars than in the past.

Car use rules

How cars are chosen for loading and how they can be used varies by the car type and who owns them. The governing instructions for this are in the Code of Car Service Rules, published by the AAR (Circular OT-10, September 2018).

These rules have evolved over time, in part because of the reduction in number of railroads. In the early 1960s there were more than 100 Class I railroads in North America; this number has dropped to five. Historically, car rules state that foreign-road cars should be used first for loading to off-line destinations, preferably to a destination on the owning, or home, road, via the home road, or at least toward the home road.

Most cars received a set per-diem (daily) fee paid to its owner by the railroad where they resided (with some privately owned cars, this was a mileage charge) as of midnight each day. This has evolved significantly, and the current standard is a mileage charge plus an hourly fee, both of which are calculated based on the value and age of the freight car.

Car owners can program the UMLER (Universal Machine Language Equipment Register, the North American database of all revenue-service cars) listing with various codes that instruct other railroads what to do with cars once they've been unloaded. This can include returning the car to its owner via the reverse route, or specifying whether the car may be given a new load without the owner's permission. It can specify that a new load may be unrestricted for destination, or that the load must be to or via the home railroad.

For cars assigned to a specific shipper or commodity pool, cars are returned to the shipper via the reverse route of the loaded movement (or per the owners' instructions).

Unassigned cars can be returned to the home railroad at any junction, or to the delivering road where the previous load was received.

Common features

Regardless of car type, some spotting features, details, and equipment are common for all cars. Trucks and brakes, covered in Chapter 10, are found on all cars, but variations and options are available to buyers.

Regulations have changed through the years. For example, the elimination of running boards on house cars in 1966 meant the elimination of full-height ladders on most cars and the lowering of brakewheel assemblies from roof level to lower on the car ends.

Other hardware and safety equipment required on all cars include side and end grab irons and/or ladders, uncoupling levers, stirrup steps, and specific types of couplers on cars carrying hazardous materials.

CHAPTER TWO

Covered hoppers

1. Covered hoppers have become the most-common car type in service. This 5,200-cubic-foot, 110-ton grain car, owned by BNSF, was built by Gunderson in 2012. It has three bays with gravity outlets. It's similar to the Trinity 5,161-cf car at left. *Cody Grivno*

In a period of less than 50 years, covered hoppers evolved from being a specialty car to the most common freight car type on the rails today. Developed initially to haul bulk cement and sand, the transition in grain business from boxcars drove the number of covered hoppers from 55,000 in 1955 to 250,000 in 1978 and more than 500,000 today, **1**.

Covered hoppers today make up about 26 percent of the total freight car fleet, with almost three-quarters of them privately owned.

Specialized covered hoppers have evolved to carry hundreds of products, with grain the most common commodity. Other common loads include plastic pellets, fertilizer, cement, sand, and potash, along with

many other powdered, granulated, and pelletized products such as carbon black, talc, powdered clay, powdered/granulated chemicals, lime, sugar, flour, starch, and soda ash.

History and design
Covered hoppers had their beginnings in the 1930s, with small two-bay cars carrying powdered cement. As with

many other moisture-sensitive bulk products, until that time cement had been typically carried in boxcars—for cement, usually in 100-pound sacks. Specialized carbon black cars followed shortly.

The success of these cars led to larger cars by the late 1950s for carrying fertilizer, potash, and sand. However, the true boom in hopper

The ACF Center Flow four-bay 5,800-cf covered hopper is a common plastic-pellet car. This one has pneumatic outlets and was built in 1992 and is leased to Dow Chemical. *Jeff Wilson*

Spotting features

Key spotting features are car length, number of outlet bays, and cubic capacity (usually stenciled on each side, or can be looked up the ORER). Also check the roof hatch size and style and the type of outlet (gravity, pneumatic, or combination).

The basic body is usually one of three types: cylindrical, teardrop (smooth rounded sides), or flat sides with vertical posts. For post cars, check the number of posts, the post pattern (evenly spaced or staggered) the type of post, and whether the edge of the roof overhangs the sides.

For rounded-side cars, look at the joint where the side meets the roof, the width of the lower side sill, and the number of vertical panels (usually visible as weld seams), Check the cutaway at each end: does the cutout sharply follow the slope sheet, or are the joints rounded?

On the ends: Does the side sill continue through the end platform area, or step down? Check the angle of the end slope sheets, and the height at which the slope sheet meets the end. Also check the style of the end ladders and end bracing, bolsters, and jacking pads. The number and type of running-board supports are also an identifying feature.

3 Product density and car capacity

The density of any given product determines the optimum car size. Ideally a covered hopper is loaded so that when its interior is full, the weight limit has been reached but not exceeded. This list of commodities carried in covered hoppers is by no means exhaustive, but provides a good idea of why plastic pellet cars are large and sand cars are small.

Pounds per cubic foot	
Product	**Pounds**
Powdered Teflon	29
Plastic/acrylic pellets	30-45
Dried distillers grains	34
Malted barley	35
Talc	35
Flour	37
Bentonite clay	37
Sunflower seeds	39
Soybean meal	40
Corn starch	43
Sugar, granulated	45
Corn	45
Wheat	49
Soybeans	50
Phosphate fertilizer	60
Soda ash	64
Potash	80
Pulverized limestone	85
Cement	94
Silica sand	96

cars wouldn't come until they began carrying grain—which wouldn't happen until the 1960s.

Covered hoppers are identified by their capacity in cubic feet, so a 4,750-cf car is known as a 4750, and so on. These numbers are sometimes rounded up or down, either by the manufacturer or owner, so a 5,701-cf car may simply be called a 5700.

They are further identified by the number of compartments and outlet bays: typically two for small cars, three for grain cars, and four for large plastic pellet and chemical cars.

Most covered hoppers built starting in the early 1960s were 100-ton cars, with 110-ton cars built since 1995.

The wide range of sizes reflects the density of the many products carried. For example, silica sand weighs almost 100 pounds per cubic foot, so it will hit the weight limit of a 110-ton car with much less volume than plastic pellets that weigh 30 pounds per cubic foot, **2**.

The chart in **3** shows the density (in pounds per cubic foot) of many common commodities, so you can get a rough idea of what will match the load limit in a 100- or 110-ton car. Remember that specific product weights vary, as do load limits based on a car's light weight (explained in Chapter 1).

Cars are broadly known by their type of service, such as a grain hopper, cement

hopper, or plastics hopper. Keep in mind that some car types can carry a variety of products, so even though a car might be referred to as a grain car, it might be equipped for and assigned to carry potash, phosphates, or soda ash.

Grain revolution

Railroads have historically been averse to acquiring specialized cars that could only be used for single commodities, as they often spend at least half their time running empty. From the early 1900s, for example, refrigerator and tank cars were almost all privately owned.

To make covered hoppers viable, railroads had to get a combination of shipping rates and a high-

Southern's aluminum jumbo "Big John" cars led the way toward the shift from boxcars to covered hoppers for hauling grain. Magor built this 4,948-cf car in **1962.** *John Ingles; J. David Ingles collection*

The Pullman-Standard 4,427-cf car was one of the most popular early grain cars. This early ("low-side," 4-3-4 post pattern) car, built in 1964, has a single long trough hatch. *Pullman-Standard*

The revised 4427 has 13 side posts. On this "high-side" car, much more of the outlet bays and center sill are visible. This car, leased to Louis-Dreyfus, was built in 1966. *John Ingles, J. David Ingles collection*

enough volume of service to make it worthwhile. For cement, the savings of hauling loads in covered hoppers versus sacks in boxcars made this possible, but for grain, it was not.

Even though the large covered hoppers in service by 1960 could carry more grain than a boxcar—and loading and unloading were much simplified—there was no rate incentive to do so. Boxcars were readily available and could be used for many other products when not hauling grain. The catch was that railroads at the time were prohibited from simply offering better rates for shipping in the larger cars, as the ICC had final approval for all interstate rates.

The car that broke the barrier was the 100-ton, four-bay aluminum covered hopper—dubbed Big John—built in 1960 by Magor for Southern Railway, **4**. It was the first car built specifically for carrying grain, and its 4,713-cubic-foot capacity meant it could carry more than twice as much as a 40-foot boxcar.

The Southern offered shippers who loaded more than five of these cars a significantly better rate than with boxcars, which still allowed the railroad to finance the cars and make money. However, in 1961 the ICC stepped in and nixed the rate following complaints from truckers and barge companies. It took multiple appeals that progressed to the U.S. Supreme Court, but the Southern finally prevailed, and a 1963 ruling finally allowed the railroad to cut rates to the level it wanted for the new cars.

The new rates were low enough that railroads—usually reluctant to invest heavily in specialized freight cars—suddenly had an incentive to acquire fleets of the new cars. The cars were almost universally accepted by shippers, as both loading and unloading were accelerated and simplified.

Along with railroads, large shippers quickly began to buy or lease their own fleets of cars, seeing the advantage that they would be available whenever they needed them without depending upon railroads. (See "Leased and private-owner cars" on page 25).

The Big John cars started a trend,

but had a unique appearance not repeated by other builders. They were 58'-11" long, 14'-8" tall, and had external side posts in a 4-3-3-4 pattern. The first order in 1960 was for 75 cars, followed by 200 additional cars (4,948-cf) in 1961-62 and 500 more (5,325-cf) in 1965. The first two orders had round roof hatches with a centered running board; the last cars were 3 feet longer and featured center trough hatches, which had become standard on all grain cars.

By the early 1960s, two companies dominated covered hopper production: Pullman-Standard and ACF. Each offered cars in multiple sizes, with several options regarding hatches, outlet bays, and number of compartments.

Both companies redesigned their cars in the early 1960s as size increased, 100-ton cars became more common, and grain transitioned to covered hoppers.

Pullman-Standard grain cars

The basic appearance of P-S covered hoppers dated back to the introduction of its all-welded PS-2 covered hopper in 1954. The car had flat sides with vertical exterior posts for strength, and was built in various lengths in two- and three-bay versions.

The key change for grain service was the adoption of a single bottom outlet gate that could dump between the rails, as opposed to earlier cars that had pairs of gates (one on each side of the center sill). The new design was termed PS-2CD, for "Center Discharge," **5**. The car still had a through center sill (a steel center sill that passed through the car), but it was angled on top to keep product from collecting atop it.

Cars of this basic design would be built until the end of Pullman-Standard in 1984, and subsequently by Trinity after it acquired P-S. Other manufacturers would also build similar cars. The key spotting features for P-S covered hoppers are the number and arrangement of vertical side posts and the height of the sides, with side sills that extend straight across the sides of the end platform.

Pullman-Standard's first true grain

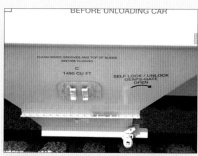

Gravity outlet

MicroMatic (pneumatic) outlet

Hopper outlets

The bottom of each compartment angles toward a bay and outlet at the bottom. Early cars had pairs of outlet doors for each compartment, with a door on each side of the center sill. Starting in the early 1960s, most cars were built with single centered outlets at each location.

Outlets on each car are one of three basic types: Gravity, pneumatic, or combination gravity/pneumatic. Each has multiple variations. Grain, fertilizer, and sand cars most commonly have gravity outlets as on the Trinity car at left. Instead of doors at angles (like coal and aggregate open hoppers), these have flat plates that cover rectangular outlets. These gates use a rack-and-pinion system where a crank is turned to slide the plate out of the way, allowing the product to fall out of the opening by gravity. 24" x 30" outlets are common, but the size can vary by intended commodity.

Pneumatic outlets have horizontal pipes mounted across each outlet. On most, the hopper bottom ends in a narrower V shape at the outlet pipe; on others, like the Micro-Matic outlet on the P-S car (top right), have a boxy appearance. A hose is connected to the end of the outlet pipe for unloading, and air pressure or a vacuum is applied to force the lading out. These are used on plastic pellet cars and cars carrying easily contaminated loads such as flour, sugar, or pelletized or powdered chemicals.

A variation of the pneumatic outlet is the fluidized (or fluidized-butterfly) outlet. These apply air at the lower sides inside the outlet bay, which fluidizes the lading to make it flow more freely without having to apply internal air pressure. Yet another variation is the sparger outlet, which allows unloading in slurry (wet) form, used for many clay cars.

Combination gravity-pneumatic outlets (right) look like a standard gravity outlet, but with a horizontal pipe below the bay. They can be unloaded by either method.

Gravity-pneumatic outlet

car debuted in 1962: a 4,000-cf version of the PS-2, which introduced the center discharge feature. The car also introduced trough-style hatches, which would become standard for grain cars (although many of these cars were also built with round hatches). These cars had tall sides and 4-3-4 post pattern.

This car was superseded in 1964 by a larger car that took advantage of the updated 263,000-pound-GRL limit: the 4,427-cf PS-2CD, **5**. The early versions of this car looked nearly identical to the 4,000-cf cars, with a

4-3-4 post pattern, but the 4427 was a foot longer (50'-7") and 2" taller.

When it was realized that the tall side walls weren't needed for strength, P-S altered the design of the 4427. Starting in 1966, the low edge of the side wall was moved upward, revealing more of the angled sides of the bays, **6**. The post pattern also changed, with 13 evenly spaced side posts.

The design saved about 800 pounds of tare weight. The new cars were termed "high-side" cars, and the earlier 4427s were termed "low-side" cars.

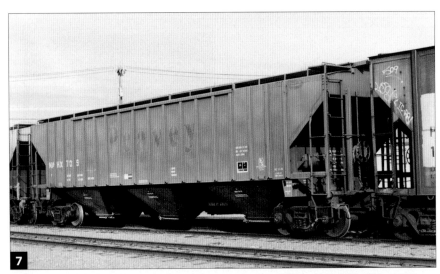

7

Pullman-Standard's most-popular grain car was the 4,750-cf PS-2CD. This 1979-built car is a late version, with an angle across the middle 12 side posts.

Jeff Wilson collection

8

Trinity's exterior-post hoppers followed P-S designs, including this 5,127-cf car. Trinity's had larger jacking pads (above the truck at each end). *Jeff Wilson*

9

The first ACF Center Flow cars had round cross sections. This six-bay, 4,000-cf car was built in 1962 for Detroit & Toledo Shore Line.

John Ingles; J. David Ingles collection

More than 10,000 low-side and about 13,000 high-side cars built. Next came the larger 4,740-cf car, which can be readily identified by its 16 evenly spaced side posts. These were built from 1966 to 1972.

After this came the most-popular PS-2, the 4,750-cf. It remained in production from 1972 to 1981. A total of 56,000 were built, with thousands still in service in the late 2010s. The 4750 can be identified by its 18 evenly spaced side posts, **7**. Notches began appearing at the bottom of each side post in 1973. In 1979, a hole appeared in the center sill between the outlet bays, and many cars received a horizontal angled strip across the top of the middle 12 side posts, as on the car in the photo.

Trinity in the late 1970s was building 4,750-cf cars that closely resembled the P-S designs, but they had a different roof cross-section (flat slopes on either side of a flat middle) compared to the rounded roof with elevated trough center of P-S cars.

When Trinity took over P-S designs in 1984, it continued offering cars based on earlier P-S cars. It built a 4,750-cf car, then expanded it to 4,870-cf, 5,127-cf and then 5,161-cf with the change to 286K GRL, **8**. Both of the larger cars had 18 side posts and resembled the 4750, but the 5127 was 6" taller (noticeable when looking at the ends) and the 5161 was also 9" longer. The Trinity cars had larger jacking pads (angled on one side) compared to the P-S design. By the late 1990s, production had shifted almost entirely toward rounded-side cars.

ACF, ARI Center Flow grain cars

ACF's early 1960s redesign was radical. Its new Center Flow car introduced curved sides for strength, allowing elimination of the center sill (much like a tank car). This allowed each bay/compartment to have a single centered outlet (hence the car name) with no sill in the way. Introduced in 1961, the first cars were nearly cylindrical, **9**.

They had capacities of 3,500- or 3,960-cf (sometimes rounded to 4,000),

10

The first ACF "teardrop" Center Flow appeared in 1964. ACF's most-popular grain car was the 4,650-cf, three-bay Center Flow, built through 1982. This early one, built in 1964, has a single upper side stiffener. *John Ingles; J. David Ingles collection*

with three or six outlet bays. Although they looked like tanks, they had slope sheets at each end, but covered by the sides and end. These cars were built until 1966.

To increase capacity without stretching length, ACF redesigned the car with flatter sides and extended the ends of the hopper bays outward, over the end platforms and trucks. ACF called its new Center Flow design a "teardrop" cross section.

The first production car of this design was a 5,250-cf, 100-ton, four-bay car for plastic pellets, introduced in 1964. Other sizes and versions shortly appeared.

The ends of the sides on the teardrop-style cars have cutouts that start out vertical and then angle to follow the slope sheet on top, **10**, with a rounded fillet where it meets the end wall, and rounded again at the bottom where it meets the platform. Spotting features include the number of outlet bays, type and number of roof hatches, angle and height of the end slope sheets, and the number of vertical (welded) side panels.

Cars built until August 1970 have a single horizontal stiffener angle running the length of the car toward the top of each side. Later cars instead have a horizontal beaded or corrugated strip where the side meets the roof, **2**.

The higher-capacity teardrop Center Flow quickly became more popular than the cylindrical version for grain.

11

This ARI Center Flow through-sill car, built in 2005, has a 5,200-cf capacity. Note how the side sill steps down at the end platforms. *Jeff Wilson*

The 4,650-cf car (53'-11" long, 15'-6" tall), **10**, appeared in 1964 and became the company's most popular grain car. About 16,000 were built through 1982. Most, like the New York Central car in the photo, had gravity outlets, but some were also outfitted with pneumatic outlets for chemical and pellet service.

The 4650 was a Plate C clearance car, and for customers looking for a similar car that would fit the tighter Plate B clearance, ACF offered a 4,460-cf version that was almost identical but not as tall (15'-1" extreme height). Another Plate B option was a 4,600-cf car that was longer and lower (55'-5" long, 15'-1" tall) than the 4650. About 15,000 were built through 1981. Yet another version was a 4,700-cf car, which looked like

the 4600 but had shallower end sheets. All were 100-ton (263,000 GRL) cars.

The move to 110-ton (286K) cars in 1995 meant an increase in cubic capacity. Although other companies have taken over much of the covered hopper business, current grain-car offerings from American Railcar Industries (ARI; the ACF subsidiary that began building Center Flow cars in 1994) include a 5,201-cf (56-foot) car and a 5,200-cf car with a through center sill (60-foot), **11**.

The ARI cars have the familiar corrugated horizontal stiffener of late ACF Center Flow cars, but their side sills step downward at the end platforms, whereas ACF cars had sills that travel straight through the end platforms.

12 Thrall built this 4,750-cf car for Soo Line in 1971. It has a 5-4-5 post pattern, and the end posts are U-channels. It has three combination gravity/pneumatic outlets.
R.J. Wilhelm; J. David Ingles collection

13 FMC covered hoppers, like this Burlington Northern 4,700-cf car, can be identified by the horizontal groove running the length of the middle of each side. *Jeff Wilson*

14 The Evans/USRE 4,780-cf covered hopper has a 5-4-5 post pattern. The sides are tall, with a straight side sill through the end platform. You can see the corrugated roof panels in this view. *R.J. Wilhelm; J. David Ingles collection*

15 The Ingalls Shipbuilding 4,750-cf covered hopper has an eave overhanging the tops of the 18 side posts. This one is in North American's lease fleet. *Jeff Wilson*

Other 100-ton grain cars

ACF and P-S dominated the grain-car market into the 1970s, but several other builders began building significant numbers of covered hoppers in the 1970s. Thrall built a 4,750-cf car that initially had a 6-4-6 post pattern, **12**.

Later Thrall cars had 16 evenly spaced posts, giving them a very similar appearance to the P-S car. Thrall's side sills step down at the end platform, giving the car a slightly different look. The end posts were U channels on many early Thrall cars (as on the Soo car in the photo), but changed to conventional posts on late cars.

FMC built grain cars in three variations from 1971 to 1981. All were three-bay cars that had tall sides and—the key spotting feature—a horizontal groove running the length of the center of the car behind the posts. The most popular was the 4,700-cf car, which had 16 side posts, **13**. The 4,692-cf car had a 5/4/5 post pattern and the 4,526-cf car a 4-3-4 pattern.

Evans (U.S. Railway Equipment) built 4,780-cf covered hoppers, identified by their 5-4-5 post pattern, tall sides, corrugated roof panels, and straight sills at each end, **14**. More than 4,000 were built from 1977 to 1981.

Ingalls Shipbuilding built 4,750-cf cars under contract to North American, **15**. These have 18 evenly spaced side posts and car-length eaves that extend over the tops of the posts. The sides are shallow, with prominent bays, and there's a pronounced step down to the end platform. About 4,000 were built.

Richmond Tank Car's 4,750-cf car resembles the Ingalls car. It also has overhanging eaves, steeply stepped end sills, arched roofs, and 18 or 19 side posts (evenly spaced on some cars; uneven on others).

In spite of the success of Southern's original Big John cars, aluminum didn't catch on in great numbers for subsequent covered hoppers. However, Magor built more than 3,000 aluminum 4,750-cf cars for several buyers through the 1970s. These have a 5-4-5 post pattern, **16**.

Other builders of 4,750-cf (or similar) cars included General American, Portec, Union Tank Car, Illinois Central,

Magor built 4,750-cf aluminum covered hoppers through the late 1960s. Many, like this 1966-built car leased to Morton Salt, were left unpainted. *J. David Ingles collection*

Norfolk & Western, Penn Central, and Union Pacific. Evans and North American also built 4,750-cf cars from kits supplied by Pullman-Standard. These cars are difficult to spot without a roster compared to true P-S cars.

A later, larger aluminum car was the Johnstown-America Grainporter, **17**, a 100-ton, 5,400-cf car. About 1,000 were built from 1994 to 1996. It's easily spotted by its smooth, flat sides with rivets outlining the slope sheets. Its tare weight is about 5 tons less than a contemporary 4,750-cf steel covered hopper. Although built as 263K cars, they were converted to 286K cars.

286K grain cars

As production shifted to 110-ton cars (286,000 pounds GRL) in 1995, manufacturers redesigned cars with increased cubic capacity. Other than the Trinity post-side cars mentioned earlier, almost all 286K grain cars have curved sides.

Trinity's curved-side 5,161-cf car, **18**, has been the most popular grain car since its introduction in 1995, with more than 27,000 built. It has been used in other services as well.

The three-bay car has rounded fillets in the cutout angles at the ends, a

The Johnstown-America Grainporter was a mid-1990s attempt at a lightweight aluminum grain car. Cargill was the major buyer of the 5,400-cf car. *Jeff Wilson*

The Trinity 5161 has been the most popular 286K grain car. It has straight side sills through the ends, rounded end cutouts, and a narrow ridge at the side/roof joint. *Jeff Wilson*

NSC's 5,155-cf car has sharp angles at the end cutouts and a stepped sill like the ARI car, but a wide, smooth ridge where the roof meets the side. *Jeff Wilson*

Thrall built this 5,150-cf car. Note the heavy, straight side sill and angled corrugated piece at the roof/side joint. *Jeff Wilson*

Cars for dried distiller's grains (DDGs) are larger than grain cars and can look at first glance like plastics cars, but they have four gravity outlets. This is a 6,350-cf NSC car. *Jeff Wilson*

The Trinity 4,197-cf car is designed for potash and similar medium-density products. This 286K car has three gravity outlets and is owned by American Soda, LLP. *Jeff Wilson*

distinctive lip where the roof overhangs the sides, and a narrow side sill that extends straight through the end platform area. The cars have eight or ten full-width welded side panels (plus the end panels with the cutouts).

Trinity also offers a 5,461-cf version of the car. Its appearance is similar, but it's about 5 feet longer and has 12 side panels.

National Steel Car's 5,155-cf car is also popular, **19**. It has a similar appearance to the Trinity car, but with sharp angles (no curves) at the end cutouts, stepped side sills, and a wider flange where the side meets the roof. NSC has also built similar cars of 4,850, 5,116-, 5,200-, and 5,300-cf capacity.

Thrall built a 5,150-cf car for several years prior to its purchase by Trinity in 2001, **20**. Thrall's car has a heavy, straight side sill, corrugated horizontal top member where the side meets the roof, and a cutout angle at each end that doesn't match the slope sheet.

Gunderson/Greenbrier's latest offering is a 5,200-cf car, **1**, with a heavy side sill that thins at the end platform, and the angle at the end cutouts is curved. It has a rounded roof that's quite pronounced, with a distinctive two-piece horizontal stiffener (three-piece on older cars) that runs the length of the car at the side/roof joint. The company has also built 5,188- and 5,250-cf grain cars.

Trinity makes a modern exterior-post aluminum car, a 5,380-cf, 286K covered hopper. It has 13 side posts and has a light weight of 56,000 pounds, about 6,400 pounds lighter than the company's popular 5161 steel car.

A variation on the grain car is the dried distillers' grain (DDG) car, used to carry spent corn from the ethanol distilling process, **21**. These cars look like grain cars, but because DDG is a finely ground product that's less dense than corn or grain, DDG cars are larger than grain cars—typically around 6,300 cubic feet.

Because the product has a tendency to clump, these cars have a fourth gravity outlet. These cars are also used for carrying seeds and other light-density agricultural products. Along with the NSC 6350 car shown in **21**, others built include the Trinity 6351 and Thrall

23 This four-bay, 4,550-cf cylindrical car was built in 1981. It was owned by the province of Alberta and assigned to Canadian Pacific. *Trains magazine collection*

6240.

Another variation on the basic grain car are smaller three-bay cars ranging from 3,200- to 4,200-cf for medium-density products like potash, fertilizer, salt, and many chemicals. These are distinctive as they're noticeably shorter than grain cars. They include the NSC 4300 and Trinity 4191, **22**.

Canadian cylindrical cars

Canadian railroads and the Canadian government began buying 100-ton cylindrical covered hoppers for grain and potash service starting in 1965. The cars, built by Hawker Siddeley, Marine Industries, and National Steel Car, resemble early Center Flow cars.

Early cars (through 1975) are mainly four-bay cars with 3,400- (50-foot), 3,800- or 3,850-cf (52-foot) capacity. Most have four cylindrical roof hatches although some have trough hatches. They were used for both grain and potash.

Higher-capacity cars began appearing in 1973. These 59-foot cars were initially 4,100-cf but most are 4,550-cf capacity, **23**. They are four-bay cars with trough hatches, and were built through 1985.

The newer cars were owned by the province of Alberta, the Canadian Wheat Board, and Saskatchewan Grain Car Corporation. They were assigned to either Canadian National or Canadian Pacific, with an N (CN)

24 Pullman-Standard built this 2,600-cf, 100-ton car for Detroit & Mackinac in 1964. The two-bay car has end sheets that don't reach all the way to the car ends. *John Ingles; J. David Ingles collection*

or P (CP) in their reporting marks indicating their railroad assignment.

Sand and cement cars

By the early 1960s, short two-bay, 70-ton covered hoppers were typically around 2,000-cf capacity, but these would soon give way to 100-ton versions. Two-bay cars were not built in as large numbers as grain cars, and were typically built in smaller lots. They were also built in a wide variety of cubic-capacity variations.

As with grain cars, P-S and ACF dominated the market through the

1970s, with the basic car designs following those of their larger cars. Many size variations were offered, from 2,800 to 3,200 cubic feet. Most have gravity outlets, but this can vary depending on cars' assigned service.

The Detroit & Mackinac car in **24**, built in 1964, shows typical P-S characteristics. The 100-ton, 2,600-cf car has a 4-4 post pattern, and the slope sheets don't extend to the end of the framework—they meet the vertical end sheet inside of the end framing.

A popular 100-ton X-post car was built by Greenville starting in

25

The Greenville (later Trinity) covered hopper was distinctive and popular. The 100-ton car had 10 side posts and slope sheets that reached all the way to the car ends. This Katy car was built in 1988. *Jeff Wilson*

26

ACF built this 3,200-cf, 263K car in 1991. It follows typical contemporary Center Flow design. This one has a pair of gravity-pneumatic outlets. *Jeff Wilson*

27

Center Flow cars are still being built by ARI. Note the stepped end platform compared to the ACF car in 226. This is a 3,272-cf, 286K car. *Jeff Wilson*

Roof hatches

Early covered hoppers featured individual round or square roof hatches. ACF used square hatches into the 1960s, but most others had become round, with openings of 20" and 30" most common. Hatches were initially placed in pairs on either side of a centered running board that ran the length of the car, generally four hatches per compartment. These hatches seal well, doing a good job of protecting lading.

In 1962, cars in grain service began receiving long trough openings down the center, with running boards to either side. This made continuous loading possible at elevators. Although some early cars had a single full-length hatch cover, most used hinged rectangular hatches that overlapped each other—generally four per car.

Round individual hatches have moved to a center location as well. They continue to be used on cars carrying easily contaminated lading, such as cement, sugar, and flour. Plastic-pellet, chemical, and food-product cars typically use smaller (20") hatches.

28

This two-bay, 3,250-cf car was built by Gunderson in 2014. It has a stepped sill, single-width stiffener at the roof joint, and curved notches at the ends. *Cody Grivno*

1981, and continued by Trinity when it acquired Greenville in 1986, **25**. The 3,000-cf car has 10 side posts, a drop where the sides meet the end platforms, and the slope sheets meet the ends very close to the roof. There was also a slightly larger version (3,317-cf) for clay service, which had 12 side posts.

Other builders of post-side two-bay cars included Portec, Evans, FMC, and Bethlehem.

ACF built a two-bay, 3,200-cf version of its teardrop-style Center Flow as a demonstrator in 1965, but production cars didn't appear until 1967. Common early two-bay cars included 2,700-, 2,960-, and 2,970-cf. Cars with 2,980-cf capacity appeared after 1976, with 3,200-cf cars by the 1990s, **26**.

Spotting features are the same as with larger ACF cars, including the single horizontal side stiffener on early cars, the wider corrugated seam on later cars, and a single seam on some long cars.

With the coming of 286K cars in 1995, cubic capacity has increased, with ARI still offering a similar car (with a through center sill, stepped end sill, higher side sill, and different end

29

This NSC 3220 has squared-off notches for ladder mounting at each end. The sill continues straight at the end platforms. The car was built in 2006. *Cody Grivno*

bracing) as with the 3,272-cf car in **27**.

By the shift to 286K cars, most manufacturers were also offering curved-sided two-bay cars, including the Trinity 3281, Thrall 3250, Gunderson 3250, **28**, and NSC3220, **29**. Most have the same basic design as the company's longer cars.

Trinity also built a 286K, 3,601-cf, two-bay aluminum car for salt service.

Plastic-pellet cars

The largest covered hoppers carry plastic (and other molding) pellets, a low-density, lightweight material

used for injection-molding a variety of products. This industry has grown tremendously since the 1960s, resulting in expanding fleets of these cars.

Built by several manufacturers, plastics cars are typically four-bay cars with pneumatic outlets. They also can carry other light-density powdered, granulated, or pelletized products, and often have lined interiors to enable the product to flow more freely, or in the case of chemical pellets, protect the walls.

Among the first dedicated plastics cars was the ACF 5,250-cf Center

The 5,701-cf Center Flow has eight visible side panels (plus end cutouts) and four pneumatic outlets. It has a wide, smooth upper-side stiffener instead of the traditional ACF corrugated stiffener. *Jeff Wilson*

ARI offers this 6,224-cf, four-bay Center Flow car for plastic pellets. The car has straight side sills and a corrugated stiffener between the roof and side.
Cody Grivno

This four-bay P-S 5,820-cf car was built in 1974. It follows contemporary P-S construction, and has 19 unevenly spaced side posts.
R.J. Wilhelm; J. David Ingles collection

Flow, introduced in 1964 and built into the 1980s. This car is 58 feet long with four outlet bays.

Additional Center Flows for plastics included the 5400 (58 feet long, introduced 1981), 5700 (or 5701) (68 feet long, later 65 feet, introduced 1968), **30**, 5800 (65 feet, introduced 1984; also listed as 5748 or 5711), **2**.

In 1990 the 6200 was introduced (62 feet long, 1990; also listed as the 6111). The current Center Flow evolution of this car from ARI is the 6224, **31**.

Pullman's first plastics covered hoppers in the 1960s were the 5400 (60-foot) and 5650 (62- or 65-foot, 1969-71) X-post cars in the 1960s, followed by the 68-foot 5820 in 1971, **32**. The first of these had 17 evenly spaced ribs; later versions had 19 ribs with slightly wider spacing among the ribs between bays; these were built through 1985.

Trinity continued offering versions of this car, but with a different ladder style, and transitioned to a 5,850-cf car through 1989. Trinity also built a similar 6150 car, but with 21 exterior posts.

Trinity changed to a rounded-side car with the 5851 in 1989, **33**. The 64-foot car has side sheets that continue all the way to the ends, across the slope sheets. A small oval cutout is located behind the top grab iron on each end; otherwise the construction resembles other Trinity covered hoppers.

Trinity now offers a 6,241-cf plastics car, **34**, a 67-foot-long, four-bay, 286K-capacity covered hopper.

Thrall began building a version of the 5800 in 1983. The 65-foot-long car resembles the ACF design, but the end cutouts have sharp angles/corners, compared to ACF's rounded corners/fillets, and there's a long, angled edge where the roof meets the side. Thrall also built a similar 6,100-cf car (3 feet longer) starting in 1989.

North American's plastics cars had a unique design, with roofs that wrapped around to the sides, a slight end angle, and side sills that tapered down to a point at each end, **35**. Sizes included 5250 and 5270 (59 feet), 5750 (64 feet), 5850 (59 feet), and 5852 (70 feet). Built from 1973 to 1980, they were also used for light-density

Leased and private-owner cars

Railroads owned most covered hoppers until the early 1960s, but shippers quickly discovered the control advantages of owning or leasing their own cars. Since the 1960s, covered hoppers have been owned by railroads, shippers, and leasing companies.

Most car builders have or had their own leasing companies, including Pullman-Standard (Transport Leasing Co., TLCX and TLDX); ACF had Shippers' Car Line (ACFX). Today, Trinity has Trinity Industries Leasing (TILX, TIMX), General American Marks Co. has the former General American fleet (GACX, GCCX), and GE Leasing has acquired the former Pullman fleet along with most of the former ACF fleet (under a variety of reporting marks).

Cars are often bought and sold second-hand as equipment trusts and leases expire. You'll find many former railroad-owned cars restenciled with reporting marks for short-line railroads or leasing companies, or vice versa.

Plastic and chemical hoppers are almost exclusively owned by shippers or leasing companies, not railroads.

33

Trinity built this 5,851-cf plastics car in 1990. It's distinctive in that it lacks end cutouts (other than notches behind the upper ladder rungs), but otherwise displays standard Trinity design. *Jeff Wilson*

34

This Trinity 6,241-cf plastics car has a wide side sill that goes through the end platforms and nine full-width side panels. The roof-side joint is standard for the builder. *Cody Grivno*

35

North American's cars were unique, with shallow angles on the ends of the sides and a taper to a point in the side sill. This 5,852-cf plastics car was built in 1973. *Jeff Wilson*

36 Among National Steel Car's latest offerings is this 6,245-cf plastics car. Note the large vertical brace centered on the end and the small notches at the top ladder rung. *Jeff Wilson*

agricultural products such as seeds.

National Steel Car began building plastics cars in 1989 with a 5,810-cf car (some are labeled 5800). The 100-ton, 67-foot car can be spotted by end cutouts that follow the slope sheet and narrow side sills compared to an ACF car. It was replaced by the 5,847 car in 1996.

The coming of 110-ton cars led to a revision of interior slope sheet angles to increase capacity to 6,245-cf, **36**. The company began offering a 6,400-cf version with the same dimensions in 2000.

Air and pressure-differential cars

Some materials don't flow as well as

37 This 4,180-cf, two-bay Airslide was built in 1974. The box-like cars have longitudinal outlet bays. Note the solid ends with horizontal braces and two rectangular lower cutouts. *Jeff Wilson collection*

38 Single-bay Airslides had open end platforms. Post-1965 cars like this 1966-built Union Pacific car had triangular end fillets, even though there was no slope sheet behind them. *Jim Hediger*

39 Pressureaide cars look like standard Center Flows, but with two sets of piping along the sides of the outlet bays. *ACF Industries*

others, and tend to clump or stick to the insides of the car during unloading. This is especially true for powdered or fine granular products. The first car to combat this using air was General American's Airslide covered hopper, first built in 1954. These cars became popular for flour, sugar, talc, starch, clay, and similar products, and about 13,000 were built into the early 1980s, **37**.

The cars use a longitudinal hopper design. The bottom of the hopper troughs are lined with Airslide fabric, a perforated, silicone-treated material. During unloading, air is pumped through the fabric, which effectively liquefies the lading at that point and allows it to flow freely to the outlet.

Airslide cars were built in short (single-bay, 2,600-cf), **38**, and long (two-bay, 3,600, 4,180-, 4,566-, and 4,900-cf) versions. The single-bay cars are 42'-6" long and have open platforms at each end. Early cars (until 1965) had diagonal braces at each end; later cars had triangular side fillets, giving them an appearance more like a conventional hopper car.

The long Airslides lack the end platforms (except for the shorter, rarer 3,600-cf car), giving them a boxy look with solid ends and solid sides with vertical posts in a 7-7 pattern.

The first true pressure-differential car—where air is introduced to force out the lading—was a series of 3,500-cf, 100-ton cars for New York Central in 1964. The railroad dubbed them Flexi-Flo cars and used them for powdered cement. The cars used 15 pounds of pressure.

In 1968 ACF modified the design to look like contemporary Center Flow cars, dropping the pressure to 5 psi (later 15 psi). The culmination of this design was branded in 1979 as the 5,000-cf Pressureaide car, **39**, again using 15 psi.

These cars can be spotted by their additional piping along the sides of the outlet bays on the left side of the car. The upper pipe is the air-supply line; the lower pipe is for unloading. In 1998, a 5,300-cf version was introduced, and the cars have also been built in 3300 and 5750 versions as 286K cars.

North American built a popular line of pressure-differential covered hoppers from the late 1960s until 1985. They carried designations of PD3000 (2,785-cf), PD4000 (3,900-cf), **40**, and PD5000 (5,150-cf). All were 100-ton cars.

The North American cars have a distinctive appearance, with cylindrical cross-section that is angled at each end, with a boxy area filling the ends. As with the Pressureaides, they have exterior piping along the outlet bays for air and unloading.

Thrall built versions of this car after acquiring the designs from NA in 1985.

Later versions of the Thrall car lack the angle at the ends, with the curved sides continuing to the end of the car, **41**. The Thrall cars have a 5,160-cf capacity.

Trinity began building a similar pressure-differential car in the late 1980s, called the Power Flo. The Trinity car was originally a 5,125-cf car, and had the same angled-end design as the NA car. The current 286K version built by Trinity is a 66-foot, five-bay 5,660-cf car, **42**. It has a stepped taper on the ends and the side-to-roof joint that resembles other Trinity covered hoppers.

North American's pressure-differential cars have a cylindrical cross section with angled, boxed-in ends and piping along the outlet bays. This five-bay PD4000 car was built in 1979. *Jeff Wilson*

Thrall modified the North American PD design to fill in the ends, eliminating the angled section and introducing a short platform. This six-bay, 5,165-cf car was built in 1996. *Jeff Wilson*

Trinity built this 5,660-cf PD car in 2004. Note the multiple angles at the ends and the two sets of side piping. This car is in the GATX lease fleet. *Jeff Wilson*

1

CHAPTER THREE

Tank cars

A string of Trinity ethanol cars trails a single locomotive and idler car on Burlington Northern Santa Fe in 2006. Modern tank cars carry a tremendous variety of products.
Jeff Wilson

From their early days of carrying mainly petroleum products, tank cars have evolved into the second most common car type, with more than 400,000 in service. Modern tank cars, **1**, carry a tremendous variety of materials, from flammable and hazardous products such as ethanol, crude oil, chlorine, anhydrous ammonia, and LPG to food products such as vegetable oil and corn syrup.

Tank car history

In the 1800s, railroads were reluctant to invest in fleets of specialized cars that had limited numbers of customers (and which would likely spend at least half their service lives running empty). Thus by the turn of the 20th century, almost all revenue-service tank cars were privately owned.

Tank car fleets were largely owned or controlled by oil companies. The largest of them, Union Tank Car (UTLX reporting marks), was initially owned by Standard Oil Co., and Union remains the largest operator of tank cars today, owning (with Canadian subsidiary Procor) about 120,000 cars.

Other major owners were car builders themselves, through their car-leasing subsidiaries. Along with Union, major lease fleets through the mid-1900s included ACF's Shipper's Car Line, General American (GATX), North American, and now Trinity, Greenbrier, and GE Leasing. Although most railroads own small fleets of tank cars, they are not in revenue service. They are used for transporting company fuel and oil products.

Tank cars were among the first all-steel cars. By 1900, they had acquired their basic familiar design, with a horizontal tank with expansion dome on top. The tank was strapped to saddles at each end of a car frame, which had a heavy center sill. The frame transmitted the slack and buffing forces of the train, with the tank merely along for the ride.

Riveted tanks eventually gave way to welded versions, first in the 1930s for high-pressure cars, then by the late 1950s for non-pressure cars.

In that decade, the growing petrochemical industry helped push a growth in the number of tank cars and the number of commodities carried. Many petroleum byproducts, additives, chemicals, and acids are carried by rail, with specialized cars and fittings for each. The food industry also began shipping more products by rail.

Modern design

The transition to modern tank car design began in 1954 when Union Tank Car built the first modern

2

This 29,000-gallon, general-purpose insulated 111S100W1 car (the "S" indicates a head shield) was built by Greenbrier in 2014. Note the ladder in a notch in the jacket. It's hauling crude oil. *Cody Grivno*

frameless car. It featured a welded tank with end sills (stub sills) and saddles welded under the tank at each end. The car had no frame or heavy center sill—instead, the tank itself transmitted all the forces of the train.

Union's design also eliminated the traditional expansion dome, instead allowing space in the tank itself for fluid expansion (called "outage"), and eliminated side running boards as well. Although Union car no. 42998 (nicknamed the HD or "hot dog" car), was revolutionary, it would take several years for railroads, shippers, and regulators to accept the idea. It wasn't until 1961 that the Interstate Commerce Commission finally approved the design.

Modern tank cars consist of a welded tank with stub sills welded to each end, **2**. Cars with aluminum tanks still have center sills, as do carbon-dioxide and cryogenic liquid cars.

A handrail/safety railing runs the length of each side between the ends of each stub sill. Most cars have vertical ladders leading to access platforms around the top manway and control valves. Brake gear is mounted either on one end above the stub sill at the end platform, or under the car.

Tank cars have shelf-style couplers, a requirement that started in 1970 (more on those in Chapter 10). These are designed to remain coupled in

Spotting features

The basic car type (insulated or non-insulated, pressure or non-pressure) is the first thing to look for, and whether the car has stub sills or a full-length center frame. Size is another key, both in the gallon capacity of the tank and also the tank length and diameter. Also look for the number of visible weld seams or courses and their arrangement. The best key in identifying the car manufacturer is often the shape and style of the saddle and stub sill (explained in the text). Other details include the style of the top manway and housing, type and location of safety valves and vents, bottom outlets and steam lines, location of brake gear, and style and location of side ladders, platforms, and handrails.

derailments, minimizing the chance of cars separating and then colliding, with a coupler puncturing the adjoining tank car end.

More than 1,600 different commodities are currently carried by tank car, with more than 90 tank car specifications. This tremendous variety in cars means this chapter can only be a rough overview of modern tank cars. We'll cover the most common variations and manufacturers.

3 Union built this 30,000-gallon general-service, uninsulated, non-pressure car in 2005. The "1987" placard on the 111A100W1 car indicates it's carrying ethanol in 2006. *Jeff Wilson*

4 ACF built this 105J500W chlorine car in 1998. It's a high-pressure, jacketed 17,300-gallon car with a single top-of-tank housing that encloses all control valves. *Jeff Wilson*

5 Some long jacketed cars, like this 66-foot LPG car, have a flat spot in the center of each side for clearance. This 33,500-gallon 105J400W LPG car, built by General American, has end access ladders. *Cody Grivno*

Basic car types

Tank cars fall into two basic categories: pressurized and non-pressurized. Non-pressure (general service) cars comprise about 75 percent of the tank car fleet, **3**. They are used for most products that are liquid at atmospheric pressure: gasoline, oil, ethanol, vegetable oil, ink, corn syrup, etc.

Pressurized cars carry gases that are liquefied under pressure (transported at more than 100 psi and up to 600 psi). The most common of these are liquefied petroleum gas (LPG), anhydrous ammonia, and chlorine, **4**. They also carry liquids classified as poison or toxic inhalation (PIH and TIH) hazards.

Cars are further categorized as insulated or non-insulated. Insulated ("jacketed") cars have insulating material covering the product tank, with a metal outer shell covering the insulation. A tell-tale sign is the tank saddles: On non-insulated cars, you'll see the saddle welded to the tank. On an insulated car, the saddle passes through the outer jacket and insulation, and will usually have a plate shielding the top of the opening.

Another giveaway on some insulated cars is a recessed area at the middle of each side. This keeps car width at the allowable dimension for a given Plate clearance. This recessed area is cut into the external jacket, not the tank itself. The car in **2** has a notch just wide

6

This 16,000-gallon insulated, non-pressure car was built by ACF in 1981. Note the lip where the jacket overlaps the end. It's owned by Occidental Chemical and is carrying potassium hydroxide. *Jeff Wilson*

7

The external jacketing and insulation has been removed from much of this General American car, revealing the actual tank with the bulges showing the external heating coils. *Jeff Wilson*

8

The large fitting in the middle is the bottom outlet; the smaller pipes on either side are connections for the steam heat coils. *Jeff Wilson*

enough for the ladder; the long LPG car in **5** has a longer notch to keep it within a Plate diagram.

Another clue is the car end: On many insulated cars, notably those built by ACF, the tank side jacketing overlaps the ends slightly, creating a distinctive lip around the end, **6**.

Non-pressure cars may be equipped with heating coils, which can be internal or external. Many liquids become thick or solidify at normal temperatures, so pumping steam (or on some cars, hot water or hot oil) through the coils warms the lading,

helping it flow better. Internal coils are located inside the tank itself. External coils are used on insulated cars. The coils are external to the lading tank, but aren't visible as they're under the outer tank shell, **7**.

Cars with heating coils have a pair of threaded pipes for connecting to a stationary steam line. Modern cars typically have these located next to the bottom outlet, **8**.

Car size

Through most of the 1950s, most general-purpose tank cars ranged from

8,000- to 12,000-gallon capacity, and were 50-ton cars. Some specialized cars for dense lading had smaller (down to 4,000-gallon) tanks, and some were larger.

Larger cars soon began appearing, enabled first by the move to 70-ton and then 100-ton cars. ACF built a 19,000-gallon, 70-ton car in 1954, and by the early 1960s, 100-ton cars with 20,000-gallon and larger tanks were being built, most featuring the new frameless, domeless design as standard.

Some specialty 70- and 100-ton cars—notably pressure cars for

Many early high-capacity cars, like this 1963-built General American 32,000-gallon pressure car, had tanks with dual diameters. The frameless car is stenciled to carry butadiene. *John Ingles; J. David Ingles collection*

This 92-foot-long car is one of five similar cars built by AMF for DuPont in early 1970. The jacketed 38,300-gallon car had a 366,000-pound load limit when built and rides on four 100-ton trucks. *L.N. Herbert; J. David Ingles collection*

Anhydrous ammonia cars are among the largest currently in service. This 112J340W car was built by Trinity in 2005. The ladder is offset to keep the center of the car within Plate C clearance limits. *Jeff Wilson*

low-density LPG and anhydrous ammonia—grew to 30,000 gallons and larger. Many of these early large cars had tanks that were smaller in diameter at the ends (above the stub sills) and larger in the middle between the trucks, taking advantage of the lack of a center sill, **9**.

These are technically "dual-diameter" cars, and were nicknamed "pregnant whales." Several thousand were built in various sizes through the 1960s, but by 1970 construction had shifted exclusively to continuous-diameter cars. A failure (complete rupture) and subsequent explosion of a 1960s-built dual-diameter LPG car in 1992 led to an inspection of about 5,000 similar cars still in service at the time. All were out of service by the 40 year mark of the newest of the cars, around 2010.

By the end of the 1960s, even larger cars were being built, including 125-ton (315,000-pound GRL) and heavier cars that either rode on six-wheel trucks or used span bolsters with a pair of four-wheel trucks at each end, **10**. Most ranged from 30,000 to 50,000 gallons. About 800 of these cars were built into 1970—most leased to petrochemical companies—and quite a few remained in service into the 2000s.

A

ACF saddle

B

ACF insulated saddle

C

Trinity saddle

D

Union saddle

E

Union insulated saddle

F

General American saddle

G

Gunderson saddle

H

North American saddle

I

Richmond saddle

Tank car saddles

Tank cars have so many variations in features that it can be hard to identify them by builder. Among the best ways to spot them (other than builders' insignia) are by tank saddles and stub sill designs.

The ACF/ARI design has a flat plate covering the side of the saddle. This plate was rectangular until the early 1980s, with newer cars having a stepped taper (wider at the bottom, narrow at the top), **A**. These plates originally went at an angle from the edge of the stub sill at the bottom all the way to the tank. Insulated cars typically have an L-angle protective strip above the opening where the saddle passes through the jacketing, **B**. Newer ARI cars have a thinner cover plate that doesn't go all the way to the top—the top of the side of the saddle is visible.

Trinity cars have a stepped saddle, **C**. A nearly vertical plate covering the side of the saddle is rectangular, but may be slightly narrower at top. There's a gap between the top of the side plate and the tank, allowing for an opening in the saddle (a "lifting eye").

On most Union-built cars, a tube covers the edge of the saddle, **D**, although on some cars this is a narrow flat piece. Insulated cars have the same design, but with a rectangular shroud covering the top, **E**.

General American saddles have a side plate that angles outward, with a thin saddle extending down to the end of the bolster and a tube going upward from the plate to the tank, **F**. There are other variations on GA cars, but they're a unique design that is hard to confuse with others.

Saddles on Gunderson/Greenbrier cars have rectangular edge pieces that have a stepped angle upward from the bolster toward the tank, split by a thin metal vertical piece at the top, **G**.

North American cars, **H**, have a wide rectangular piece extending down from the tank that meets an angled piece coming upward from the end of the bolster.

Richmond/GRI cars have a wide rectangular end cover that's nearly vertical from the end of the bolster upward to the tank, **I**.

Concerns about safety, as well as train handling, led to tank car size regulations that ended production of jumbo cars. In November 1970 the DOT capped tank car size at 34,500 gallons and 100-ton capacity (263,000 pounds GRL), effective for cars built after November 1971. Since the adoption of the 286,000-pound GRL in 1996, some non-hazardous-material 110-ton cars are now allowed.

Today, the largest tank cars are the 33,000- to 34,500-gallon pressure cars carrying light-density products, mainly LPG and anhydrous ammonia, **11**. Chlorine cars have a similar appearance, but are shorter, with tanks around 17,000 gallons.

Cars are built in a wide range of gallon capacities. Light-density liquids such as alcohol (including ethanol), gasoline, crude oil, and lube oil are commonly carried in cars from 25,000 to 30,000 gallons, **2, 3**.

12

Trinity built this 17,600-gallon insulated, coil-equipped corn syrup tank car in 1996. To match loading platforms, the AAR211A100W1 car has a 6" larger tank diameter than most other tank cars. *Jeff Wilson*

13

Hydrochloric acid weighs about 9 pounds per gallon, and is typically carried in tank cars of medium size. ACF built this non-insulated, 20,830-gallon car in 2002. Acid cars lack bottom outlets. *Jeff Wilson*

14

Union built some very small tank cars in the late 1960s, like this 10,000-gallon car, dubbed "beer can" cars. They were a standard diameter, allowing them to be easily rebuilt to longer cars if needed. *Stan Mailer*

High-density products, such as sulfuric acid (and many other acids and chemical compounds), molten sulfur, caustic soda, and corn syrup, travel in smaller cars with 14,000- to 18,000-gallon capacities, **12**.

Medium-density commodities, including vegetable oils, asphalt, hydrochloric acid, and many other chemicals, are loaded in 20,000- to 25,000-gallon cars, **13**.

Other than some specialty and extremely small cars (under 10,000 gallons), most builders generally used a standard tank diameter (110" or 111"), stretching it as needed to various lengths, **14**. This means car length varies considerably, with truck centers from about 27 feet apart on smaller cars to 54 feet for large cars.

Manufacturers

Primary tank car builders into the modern era included ACF, Union Tank Car (which began building its own cars in 1955), and General American. Other builders included North American, **15**, Richmond Tank Car, **16**, and Richmond successor Gulf Railcar Inc. (GRI).

Union still builds cars, both for its own UTLX leasing fleet as well as other leasing fleets and private owners. Other current tank car builders include ACF subsidiary American Railcar Industries (ARI), formed in 1994,

North American built this general-service non-pressure DOT111A100W1 car in 1973. It's shown carrying ethanol in 2006.
Jeff Wilson

Richmond Tank Car built this general-purpose 21,000-gallon car in 1971 for Pullman's leasing fleet (TLDX reporting marks).
Richmond Tank Car

Trinity, which purchased General American in 1984 (GATX still operates as a leasing company), Greenbrier, and National Steel Car (NSC).

Tank cars have so many variations in features that it can be hard to identify them by builder. Among the best ways to spot them (other than builders' insignia) are by tank saddles and stub sill designs. See "Tank saddles" on page 33 for photos and descriptions for the major manufacturers.

Loading, fittings

Most loading, unloading, and safety fittings are centered on top of the car. Non-pressure cars, **17**, have a hatch atop the tank with a hinged cover. Called a manway, this opening into the tank can be used for loading and also allows interior access for cleaning and maintenance. The cover has a series of bolts around the perimeter that are

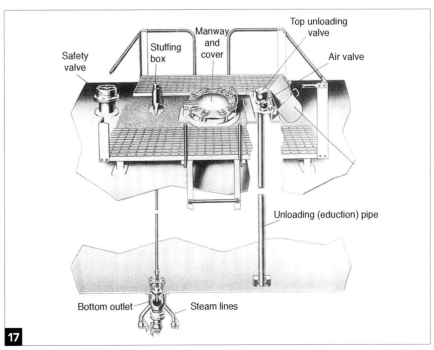

This drawing shows a typical arrangement of fittings for a non-pressure car.
GATX Inc.

tightened to seal the opening.

Loading can be done through the manway, **18**, or by using a closed-loop system that captures all vapors.

Unloading can be through the top or bottom outlet, **19**. Not all cars have bottom outlets, and some commodities (such as acids) can't be carried in bottom-outlet cars. On cars with bottom outlets, a capped, threaded pipe is located at the center of the tank bottom.

Some bottom outlets are opened and closed with a valve atop the car, called the stuffing box; others have the control handle at the bottom outlet. The valve is opened after the unloading hose or pipe has been connected to the outlet.

The top unloading controls are located under a housing that hinges open. The top unloading valve is connected to a vertical pipe (eduction pipe) that passes down to the bottom of the tank interior. Many cars have a pronounced sump—a downward bulge at the bottom center of the tank—to enable as much liquid as possible to be easily unloaded.

During unloading, the manway must be open (or an air valve on some cars) to vent air into the car. If this isn't done, the lading will empty slowly, and the vacuum created by unloading can be enough to collapse the tank.

Cars may also have a "bottom washout," a plugged opening on the bottom of the tank designed not for unloading but for access for cleaning.

On pressure cars, **20**, all of the inlet and outlet controls and connections are in a manway housing or bonnet

18
Product can be loaded directly into the manway opening, as on this ethanol car. To the right of the manway are the control housing and safety valve. *Jeff Wilson*

19
Gasoline is being unloaded from this uninsulated 21,000-gallon car via a hose connected to the bottom outlet. Note that the manway cover is propped open to allow venting. The car was built by General American. *Jeff Wilson*

at the top of the tank. Pressure cars all use closed systems for loading and unloading, as exposing the contents to atmospheric pressure would vaporize the lading.

Generally three connections (two liquid eduction and one vapor eduction) are used for commodity unloading and venting, **21**. Holes in the bonnet (normally covered by flaps) allow hose connections. The two product lines are connected toward the car ends; the vapor line is toward the side.

Non-pressure cars have one or more safety valves or vents (called pressure-relief devices, or PRDs) located next to the manway atop the car, set to the appropriate pressure for the lading. There are many variations, but they fall into two basic types: valves and vents.

Safety valves are spring-loaded and reclosing (they vent pressure if needed, then close when the pressure drops below the valve rating). Cryogenic and carbon-dioxide cars use regulating valves to keep pressure at the desired level. These cars, which continuously

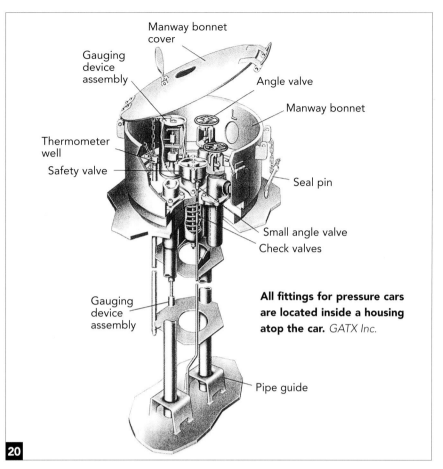

Manway bonnet cover

Gauging device assembly

Angle valve

Manway bonnet

Thermometer well

Safety valve

Seal pin

Small angle valve

Check valves

Gauging device assembly

All fittings for pressure cars are located inside a housing atop the car. *GATX Inc.*

Pipe guide

20

21

Unloading is done with two product lines (from the T stand at right) and with one air line (hose from stand at left). Connections are through openings in the manway bonnet. *Trains magazine collection*

Cryogenic tank cars have a tank within a tank—like a large Thermos bottle. This car, built in 1963, is carrying nitrogen. Note the gas being vented at the control box to the left of the ladder. *John Ingles; J. David Ingles collection*

Tank car classifications

Class	Pressure	PSI	Insulated	Description
DOT103*	N	35	Both	Tank with expansion dome
DOT104*	N	35	I	Tank with expansion dome
DOT105	P	75-450	I	Steel (carbon or stainless) tank
DOT106	P	375-600	Non	Multiple removable tanks
DOT107	P	Varies		Multiple seamless tanks
DOT109	P	75-225	Both	Carbon steel or aluminum tank
DOT110	P	375-750		Multiple removable tanks
DOT111	N	35-75	Both	Domeless steel or aluminum tank
DOT112	P	150-375	Non	Steel (carbon or stainless) tank
DOT113	—	30-115	I	Cryogenic with vacuum insulation
DOT114	P	255-300	Non	Steel (carbon or stainless) tank
DOT115	N	35	I	Insulated tank
DOT117	N	35-75	I	Upgraded version of DOT111
DOT120	P	150-450	I	
DOT211	N			
AAR203*	N	35	Both	(matches DOT103)
AAR204	—	30-115	I	(matches DOT113)
AAR206	N	35	I	(matches DOT115)
AAR207	N	—	Non	Car for granular products, pneumatic unloading
AAR208	N	—	Non	Wood-stave tank with metal hoops
AAR211	N	35-75	Both	(matches DOT111)
* Obsolete by 1980s				

vent, have stenciling that states "venting normal," **22**.

Safety vents, also known as rupture-disc devices, non-reclosing PRDs, or frangible vents, are designed to fail and rupture at a certain pressure. They are often used for corrosive materials, acids, and food products. Some cars use a combination PRD with a rupture disk coupled to a valve. With these, a rupture shows that the car has vented, but the valve recloses when the pressure drops below the rated level.

Vacuum-relief valves are used on some non-pressure cars to allow air into a tank, as with unloading.

On pressure cars, the safety valves are at higher pressure ratings compared to non-pressure cars. These are contained inside the car-top housing.

Pressure cars carrying flammable gas must have a fire-resistant thermal barrier (usually jacketed, as with an insulated non-pressure car). Unlike standard car insulation, which is designed to keep the contents at a controlled temperature, a thermal barrier is designed to protect the tank and contents from outside fire if the car is in an accident.

Some tank cars carry remote monitoring equipment, which can transmit information on location,

This 13,500-gallon car, built by Union, is in sulfuric acid service. It is lined, has no bottom outlet, and safety vents are located on the manway cover. Its AAR code is T054. *Jeff Wilson*

pressure, temperature, possible leaks, or attempted tampering. These small boxes have bright yellow or orange labels on or next to the sensor.

Classifications and variations

The Interstate Commerce Commission (ICC) was responsible for classifying tank cars from 1927 until 1967. In 1967, the Department of Transportation (DOT) took over classification duties, keeping the same numbering system and adding new ones as needed. In addition, the Association of American Railroads (AAR) provides classification specifications for cars not carrying hazardous materials.

Class numbers indicate car characteristics and the type of lading it can carry. See "Tank Car Classifications" on page 38. The most common ICC and DOT types have been 103 (general purpose, non-pressure, with dome—now obsolete), 104 (insulated, non-pressure, with dome—also obsolete), 105 (insulated, pressure, welded), 111 (domeless non-pressure, with or without insulation), and 112 (non-insulated, pressure, welded). Each of the specifications covers a wide range of car sizes, fittings, and types.

The Pipeline and Hazardous Materials Safety Administration (PHMSA) is the federal regulation agency governing hazardous shipments by rail, including all flammables by tank car. The AAR's Tank Car Committee also works (with owners, shippers, car builders, Transport Canada, and the National Transportation Safety Board) to establish tank car standards covering the North American rail network.

After several accidents involving DOT-111 tank cars, in May 2015 the PHMSA issued rulings on tank car construction as well as operation of trains carrying hazardous materials. The result was the new DOT-117 specification for tank cars, calling for thicker shells, thicker head shields, and improved valves and fittings.

Cars built beginning in October 2015 must follow DOT-117 guidelines. Existing DOT-111 cars can remain in certain types of service (with varying deadlines), but all are to be rebuilt (upgraded to 117 standards) or retired by 2025.

In 2009, the DOT revised standards for inhalation hazard (toxic-by-inhalation materials) cars, resulting in the DOT105J600I, also with thicker shells and heads and improved safety

valves and fittings. Older cars can continue in service provided they met earlier standards. Affected products include chlorine, anhydrous ammonia, sulfuric acid, and several other specified materials.

In addition, the AAR also assigns car codes to tank cars. These are a "T" (for tank car) followed by a three-digit number. The first two digits indicate the general type and the last digit is a size range. For example, a T108 is a non-pressure steel car with a capacity from 27,500 to 31,499 gallons; a T389 is a 112J340W pressure car with a capacity of at least 31,500 gallons.

Specialty cars

Along with general-purpose cars, many are built to carry a specific commodity. It's not visible from the outside, but many commodities require an internal tank lining to protect the tank from corrosion or to keep the lading from reacting with the tank material. This lining is listed with the car stenciling. Tanks may also be built using stainless steel or aluminum (instead of standard carbon steel) for some lading.

Acid cars are generally smaller lined cars (13,000 to 20,000 gallons), **23**. Acid cars don't have bottom unloading outlets. Many, like this one, have all

24

This 20,000-gallon carbon dioxide car has a frame—note the tank band at the saddle going upward into the jacketing. The 105A500W car was built by General American in 1975. *John Ingles, J. David Ingles collection*

of their loading and unloading fittings mounted atop the manway cover plate.

Cryogenic tank cars (DOT113 and AAR204) have vacuum-insulated tanks—picture a large version of a Thermos bottle, **22**. They carry refrigerated liquified gases such as argon, nitrogen, oxygen, and hydrogen, all of which have a boiling point of -130 degrees or colder.

Unlike an ordinary insulated tank car, the outer shell of a cryogenic car is a full carbon-steel tank, not a simple jacket, with an inner stainless steel tank. The control valves and PRVs are generally at one end (or side) of the car in a protective box-like housing, with no fittings atop the tank.

Carbon dioxide cars are similar, but have top fittings. These cars look like other high-pressure tank cars, but they aren't frameless, instead having a center sill between bolsters, **24**.

Non-pressure cars with sloped tanks are now common for many ladings, especially those that don't flow easily, **25**. Union introduced the concept in 1967 as the Funnel-Flow car, and other manufacturers offer similar designs, usually simply termed "slope-bottom" cars. They're made in several sizes and with varying slope angles depending on the lading being carried.

Anhydrous ammonia and LPG cars are distinctive, as they're generally the largest cars (32,000 to 34,500 gallons), 112J340W, with pressure-car fittings atop the tank. Chlorine cars are also pressure cars, and look like shorter versions of LPG and anhydrous ammonia cars (around 17,000-gallon capacity) but they have a higher pressure rating (105J500I), with the "I" indicating an inhalation hazard lading.

Corn syrup is a common commodity in the food and beverage industry. Tank cars in this service are typically 17,000 to 20,000 gallons, and they're insulated cars with external heating coils (to get the thick liquid to

25

This slope-bottom, insulated 16,000-gallon tank car was built by ACF in 2001 and is carrying limestone slurry. The AAR211A100W1 car has no safety valves. *Cody Grivno*

General American's TankTrain features tank cars connected end-to-end by flexible piping, allowing all cars in a string to be unloaded and loaded from a single point. The original cars in 1977 carried a bold paint scheme. *George Drury*

flow). Notable versions are the 110-ton (286K) cars built beginning in 1995. Major corn syrup shippers wanted the car lengths to remain the same as earlier 100-ton cars (to match existing loading and unloading platforms), so the result was a distinctive car with a fatter tank.

You can see a Trinity car in **12**, which has an outside diameter over the jacket of 125.4", noticeably larger than the 119.4" diameter of earlier 100-ton cars. Along with a squatty appearance, these have the side ladder recessed into the jacket to keep the width to Plate C dimensions.

Another notable development was the TankTrain system, introduced by General American in 1977, **26**. The system uses strings of multiple cars interconnected end to end with flexible hoses, allowing multiple cars to be loaded and unloaded from one connection.

The initial TankTrain cars were painted with large graphics as shown in the photo, but current cars look more like standard tank cars (but with the hose connections between cars). Car sizes and types (and number of cars in a string) vary based on commodity, including various petroleum products

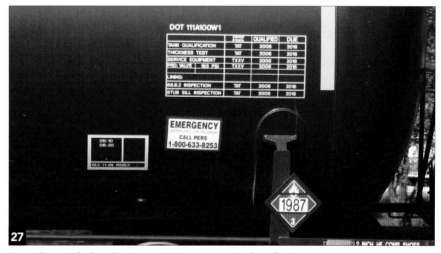

Stenciling includes the DOT, AAR, ICC, or TC classification, along with a matrix showing test dates for various equipment. *Jeff Wilson*

and chemicals. Cars generally travel in standard manifest trains.

Lettering and paint

The full tank car specification is stenciled at the top of the right side of each car, **27**. The first initials of this are the authorizing agency: ICC, DOT, AAR, or TC (Transport Canada). The next three numerals are the car's class designation (discussed earlier), which define the basic car type.

Next is the delimiter letter. For most standard cars this is "A," which has no

special meaning. A "J" means the car is equipped with a jacketed thermal protection layer and tank-head shield. An "S" means it has a tank-head shield, and a "T" means it has a non-jacketed thermal protection system and tank-head shield.

The next numerals indicate the tank test pressure (technically in PSIG, or pounds per square inch gauge). This is usually 60 or 100 for non-pressure cars, although some are tested at 165. Pressure cars range from 100 to 600 PSIG.

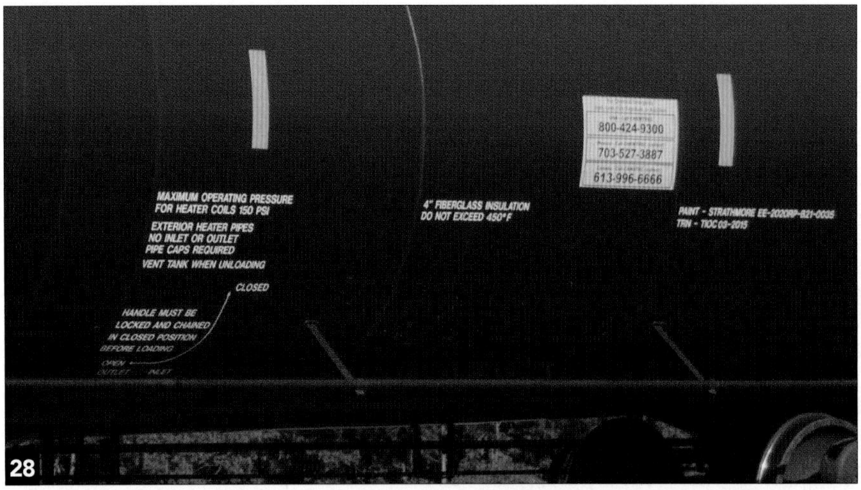
28
800-424-9300
703-527-3887
613-996-6666
MAXIMUM OPERATING PRESSURE
FOR HEATER COILS 150 PSI
EXTERIOR HEATER PIPES
NO INLET OR OUTLET
PIPE CAPS REQUIRED
VENT TANK WHEN UNLOADING
CLOSED
HANDLE MUST BE
LOCKED AND CHAINED
IN CLOSED POSITION
BEFORE LOADING
OPEN
4" FIBERGLASS INSULATION
DO NOT EXCEED 450°F
PAINT - STRATHMORE EE-2020RP-821-0035
TRN - TIOC 03-2015

Along with a yellow Chemtrec decal, this car's lettering includes information on its insulation, heater coils, and bottom outlet operation. *Jeff Wilson*

The next letter or letters indicate material and construction. A "W" is a fusion-welded steel tank and "ALW" is an aluminum tank. An "I" (as of 2009) means the car carries poison or inhalation hazard lading.

The final number indicates whether a car can have a bottom outlet or washout, and also specifies additional construction. A 3 or 4 means a car is insulated; 5 is elastomer lined, and 6 or 7 mean a stainless-steel tank. A 4, 5, or 7 cannot have bottom outlets or washouts.

Tank and valve test information is also included on the right side. As of 1998, this information is included in a standardized matrix that lists test dates and renewal dates for tank thickness and safety valve (PRD). Stub sill welds must also be periodically checked for cracks (in the sill or on the tank itself where the sill is welded). This date is also in the matrix. Initials in the boxes show the facility where inspections were performed.

Loaded cars carrying hazardous materials must carry hazmat placards on each side of the car. These are color-coded based on the type of material, and whether the material is flammable, corrosive, reactive, or an inhalation hazard. They also carry the four-digit numerical code that identifies the lading: For example, 1203 for gasoline and 1017 for chlorine. Empty cars will not carry placards.

Cars carrying many classes of hazardous materials are required to be stenciled with their lading (see **4**, **5**, **13**, **23**). Cars carrying other products are often stenciled as well. As cars are reassigned, you can sometimes see where this lettering has been painted out and new stenciling added.

Cars may carry a decal with a Chemtrec or other 800 number to report spills or accidents. Other detail lettering includes information on car lining, heating coils, paint, insulation, outlet valves and handles, loading, unloading, and cleaning, **28**.

As with other cars, tank cars have consolidated stencils on each side that include the date built and information on brake inspection and lubrication.

The reporting marks and number, load limit, and light weight are on the left of each side. The reporting marks and number and the car's capacity in gallons and liters is centered on each end.

For a brief period, Canadian-owned pressure cars carrying hazardous materials were required to carry a 12"-wide horizontal orange stripe centered around the tank (by order of Canadian Transport Commission, that country's version of the DOT in the U.S.). This was begun in the mid-1980s, with all such cars to be so marked by July 1990. However, the U.S. did not adopt this standard, and the requirement was dropped after a few years.

Since 2003, new cars are required to have a stainless-steel plate on each side at the bolster web. These plates include the car's manufacturer, serial number, date built, car specification, and other information.

Black has long been the most common color for tank cars, although non-jacketed pressure cars are required to have a light color on the top of the car. Anhydrous cars are often white. Many cars in acid service are white with wide vertical bands at the center.

Notable are cars carrying hydrocyanic acid, which have a thin horizontal red stripe centered on a white car, with thin vertical stripes above each truck (sometimes called "candy stripe" cars).

Product weight and density

Tank car size is largely based on the density of the lading it's designed to carry, with the goal of getting as close as possible to the 263K or 286K (for non-hazardous materials) GRL. Here's a list of a few products commonly carried by rail, with weight per gallon in pounds (along with water for reference). This shows, for example, why an LPG car is significantly larger than a chlorine car, even though both have the same gross rail load.

Product	Pounds/gallon
LPG	4.2
Anhydrous ammonia	5.0
Gasoline	6.0
Acetone	6.6
Ethanol	6.8
Lubricating oil	7.0
Crude oil	7.5
Corn oil	7.8
Water	8.3
Hydrochloric acid (15%)	9.0
Asphalt	9.5
Hydrogen peroxide (35%)	9.5
Chlorine	10.0
Corn syrup	11.5
Potassium hydroxide	12.1
Tetraethyl lead	14.0
Kaolin clay slurry	14.5
Molten sulfur	15.0
Sulfuric acid	15.0

CHAPTER FOUR

Boxcars

It's hard to believe that the once-ubiquitous boxcar is now a minority, representing only about 8 percent of the North American railcar fleet—behind covered hoppers, tank cars, hoppers, gondolas, and intermodal cars, **1**. And those boxcars that remain are mainly specialized cars, as the era of the general-service boxcar has almost gone away.

These 110-ton FBOX boxcars began appearing in 2003. This Trinity-built version is 50 feet long with a 12-foot plug door. Owned by TTX and operated in a pool, it's typical of modern boxcars. *Jeff Wilson*

Most boxcars are still owned by railroads—about 22 percent of boxcars today are privately owned. Boxcars, however, are as a group the oldest car type on the rails, with more than half over 30 years old as of 2015.

The AAR class for boxcars is X, with XM indicating a general-purpose car. Other common subclasses have included XF, a non-insulated, lined car specifically for food products; XL and XML for loading-device-equipped cars; XAP for auto-parts cars; and XP and XMP for cars equipped for specific commodities.

History and design

Boxcars were the dominant car type through the 1950s, carrying everything from canned goods to automobiles to bulk grain. The typical boxcar of the period was a non-cushioned, 50-ton, 40- or 50-foot car built to AAR standard designs, with a 6-foot (or perhaps 7- or 8-foot) sliding door. Automobile and auto-parts cars were often double-door cars.

Many of the first new boxcars of the early 1960s looked much like the general-purpose AAR-design cars of

2

The Burlington built this 50-foot, 70-ton car in 1963. The double-door car (15-foot opening) has roller-bearing trucks, a cushion underframe, smooth (riveted) sides, and Dreadnaught ends. *John Ingles; J. David Ingles collection*

3

Great Northern built this combination-door (plug and sliding) car in 1963. The 70-ton car features exterior-post construction, roller-bearing trucks, and uses Pullman wrap-around ends. *John Ingles; J. David Ingles collection*

Spotting features

Key spotting features for boxcars are length and height, doors (number, type, width), side construction (smooth-side or exterior-post; number and placement of posts or side panels; side sill style), end style, and roof style. Check for the style and location of ladders and grab irons, and whether the car has cushioning.

previous decades, but most were now 50 feet long. They most commonly featured smooth-side (sheet-and-post) construction, **2**.

Pullman-Standard, with its PS-1, and ACF still dominated boxcar production, with many other manufacturers building them as well. In addition, many railroads built their own boxcars through the 1960s and even later, including Burlington Northern predecessors Chicago, Burlington & Quincy, Northern Pacific, and Great Northern; Santa Fe; Soo Line; New York Central (Despatch Shops) later Penn Central and Conrail; Pennsylvania; Baltimore & Ohio; Reading; Illinois Central; and Illinois Central Gulf.

However, the era of specialized car types was dawning, and boxcars were quickly following suit. Door sizes had been growing, with width typically 8 feet or more, compared to the 6 feet of the transition era's common 40-foot general-service car. Plug doors were also becoming more common, especially for insulated boxcars (more on those in Chapter 9).

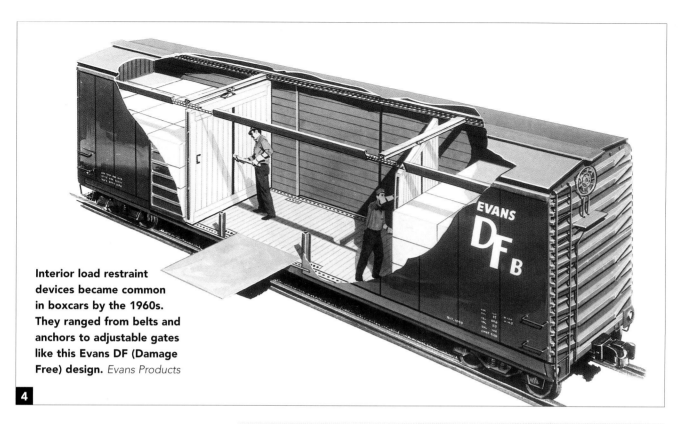

Interior load restraint devices became common in boxcars by the 1960s. They ranged from belts and anchors to adjustable gates like this Evans DF (Damage Free) design. *Evans Products*

4

Another trending arrangement was a double plug/sliding door, **3**. That car also shows the growing trend toward external-post (X-post) designs.

Car capacity and size were growing, with 70-ton (220,000-pound GRL) cars common by 1963. By that time, most new boxcars were 50 or 60 feet long, with even larger auto parts cars on the horizon.

Other common emerging boxcar features included cushioning (either end-of-car or center-of-car—more on that in Chapter 10), often noted by bold lettering on the cars: Hydra-Cushion, Shock Control, and Hydroframe were common.

Internal load restraints and dividers were also becoming common, including belts, moveable panels, and other devices, **4**. Most common were products from Evans, with variations on the company's "DF" (Damage Free) lettering often applied to cars.

Auto-parts and specialized cars

Among the earliest specialty boxcars were the distinctive 60- and 86-foot cars designed in the early 1960s specifically to carry auto parts. Both were designed with clean interiors to

Roofs

Most boxcar roofs into the 1960s were peaked, with sections separated by raised seams. These sections have raised panels or corrugations for strength, with the pattern the key spotting feature. Most common are Stanray's diagonal pattern and X-pattern, found on cars from many builders, or "bow-tie" pattern, a proprietary design from Pullman-Standard. Flat roofs became common for clearance reasons, and these patterns can be found on both types of roof.

Running boards were mandatory on roofs until 1966, except for high-cube cars, which didn't require them after 1964. Steel running boards (of various types) had been required on new cars since 1945. Running boards were then removed from cars, with an initial target date for removal from all cars by 1974, but this was extended to 1983.

Corrugated (left), diagonal-panel

X-panel

Pullman-Standard ("bow-tie")

The 86-foot auto parts cars carried light-density components. Pullman-Standard built this 263K car for Detroit, Toledo & Ironton in 1970. *R.J. Wilhelm; J. David Ingles collection*

Thrall built this smooth-side (welded) 60-foot auto parts car in 1963. The "150" above the railroad initials indicates the parts plant pool to which it is assigned.

John Ingles; J. David Ingles collection

This Union Pacific auto parts car, built by Pullman-Standard in 1963, is a 100-ton (263K GRL) car. The exterior-post, double-plug-door car has roller-bearing trucks.

John Ingles; J. David Ingles collection.

carry standardized racks that could be modified to hold many types of parts. This sped loading and unloading compared to the custom parts racks that were directly built into earlier boxcars.

Both types of these new cars were designed by committees comprising railroads, car builders, and auto manufacturers, with several manufacturers building each type of car.

The 86-foot cars were built to carry light-density parts, mainly metal stampings (fenders, body panels, etc.), 5. They became known as high-cube cars for their large interior cubic capacity, enabled because of their excess height (taller than Plate C clearance). "High-cube" soon became an accepted term for any excess-height car.

The 86-footers had either twin doors or four doors (two openings) per side. In spite of their huge size, most were still 70-ton cars, as a full load was typically only 10 to 25 tons of stampings. The first cars, in March 1964, had running boards, but subsequent orders did not—these were the first boxcars delivered without them.

Most of these high-cubes were built by Greenville, Thrall, and Pullman-

Standard, with a limited number built by Pacific Car & Foundry. The P-S cars had versions of that company's distinctive ends, and were welded. Thrall's cars were also welded (except for a few late ones), but with Dreadnaught ends. Greenville cars were riveted, and the bottom side sills were recessed. The PC&F cars were the only exterior-post versions. More than 11,000 were built through 1978.

The 60-foot auto parts cars carried heavier items such as engine components, transmissions, and axles. They were built by Greenville, ACF, Thrall, **6**, and Pullman-Standard, and several railroads also built cars as well.

There were more variations with the 60-foot parts cars than the 86-footers. Most featured sheet-and-post construction, **6**, but many were also built to exterior-post designs, **7**. Variations include roof and end styles, as well as door openings and styles. Most had 16-foot openings with double plug doors, but some had sliding doors and single 10-foot doors. All had cushioning of some type. They were built in both 70-ton and 100-ton versions.

The auto parts cars influenced other boxcar designs as well. Other specially equipped cars often followed the same basic construction, **8**.

Shorter high-cube cars also began appearing, **9**. The 40-foot, 70-ton cars were most often used in appliance service, another product that has a lot of bulk but not much weight. The tall interiors allowed stacking appliance boxes vertically.

Slightly longer high-cubes (50-footers), **10**, found their niche hauling finished lumber products (mainly plywood, particle board, and other sheet material) and paper. These typically have double-plug doors to keep the interior as clean as possible.

All-door and grain-door cars

A unique car design that emerged in the late 1960s was the all-door boxcar. These were designed principally to carry dimensional lumber and lumber products from the Northwest, and most were owned or leased by private owners. Each side had four sliding

8 Parts car design influenced other cars as well. This 60-foot St. Louis-San Francisco car, built in 1967 by Evans, has double Superior sliding doors and a hydraulic underframe. *James A. Kinkaid collection*

9 Pullman-Standard built this 40-foot excess-height car in 1967. It has a Hydroframe underframe and Evans DF2 loading devices. The Burlington assigned it to appliance service. *Hol Wagner collection*

10 This double-plug-door, waffle-side Pullman-Standard car was built in 1971 and later rebuilt. Excess-height 50-foot cars are often used to carry lumber and paper products. *Jeff Wilson*

The Thrall-Door boxcar has four doors on each side. An opening two-doors wide allowed forklift access for loading and unloading bundled dimensional lumber. *Thrall*

The Evans Side Slider can be spotted by its two door styles: plug in the middle and Superior sliding on the outside positions. This one was built in 1978.

John Ingles; J. David Ingles collection

The Burlington built 800 exterior-post, double-plug doors with grain hatches in 1964. The gray-painted panels swung open (one for loading, one for inspection).

John Ingles; J. David Ingles collection

doors, enabling any pair of doors to be open. This allowed fork trucks good access to load and unload bundled lumber.

The most popular was Thrall's design, which it tabbed the Thrall-Door boxcar, **11**. They had an inside length of 52'-5" and side doors of the same design. The cars had heavy fishbelly style underframes, since the car sides (because of the doors) didn't offer structural strength. Likewise the ends have heavy vertical posts (freight car expert Jim Eager calls them "bulkhead flatcars with doors and a roof"). Early Thrall cars have the roof extending over the ends; on later cars the roof doesn't extend as far.

Other companies built similar cars, notably the Evans Side Slider, **12**. This car was shorter, with a 50'-6" inside length, and can be spotted by its doors, which were different compared to the Thrall car. The Evans design had two plug doors in the center positions, with the outer two doors being Superior sliding doors. Pacific Car & Foundry and SIECO also each built small numbers of similar cars.

All-door cars protected their cargo well, but their complex door

Railbox cars, 70-ton, 50-foot boxcars, began arriving in 1974; this Plate B FMC car was built in 1975 and has a Youngstown door and non-terminating ends. *R.J. Wilhelm; J. David Ingles collection*

mechanisms proved to be high-maintenance items. The advent of center-beam flatcars and wrapped lumber loads doomed them, with the last all-door cars built in the late 1970s.

Another specialized design of the 1960s was the grain-door boxcar. As the number of 40-foot boxcars available for grain loading dropped, new boxcars were built with plug doors with hatches at the top, **13**. This way they could be loaded with grain without the need for separate wood or paper grain doors, but could easily be used in general service.

Burlington built 800 new cars of this type, 50-foot, 70-ton external-post cars, in 1963 and 1964, and Soo Line built 200 similar cars. Other railroads did the same but rebuilt them from older 40-foot cars, including Union Pacific (4,000 cars) and Santa Fe (450).

Railbox cars

By the early 1970s, the rise of specially equipped boxcars and the shift of many commodities away from boxcars led to a shortage—or perceived shortage—of general-purpose boxcars. Many bankrupt and struggling railroads, especially in the Northeast, were not financially able add new general-service cars to their fleets.

The first effort to combat this

Pullman-Standard built this Plate C, 5,077-cf car in 1980. It has a P-S door (note different corrugations compared to Youngstown) and narrow-corrugation non-terminating ends. *Jeff Wilson*

was Railbox, **14**. The idea came to fruition in 1973 when a group of 11 solvent Class 1 railroads agreed to finance a fleet of new 50-foot, 70-ton boxcars. The cars were managed by the American Rail Box Car Co. (later Railbox Co.), which was set up as a subsidiary of Trailer Train.

The cars, like Trailer Train's intermodal cars, were designed to be operated in a pool as "free runners"—not having a home road, but available for loads wherever needed to any destination. The first cars arrived in 1974, with about 10,000 in service

by 1978 and a total fleet of 25,000 by 1981. They wore a distinctive bright yellow scheme.

Railbox cars were built by several builders to common designs. All were external-post cars, with detail differences among builders including ends, doors, number of side posts, and side sills.

Railbox cars fall into three basic categories. The XF10 class were single-door Plate B cars, XF20 were single-door Plate C cars, **15**, both with 10-foot sliding doors. The XF30 cars were Plate C cars but with

This FMC-built ABOX car features a combination 10-foot sliding door and 6-foot plug door. The Plate C, 5,277-cf car is 5" taller than the Plate B car in 14. *John Ingles; J. David Ingles collection*

combination doors (10-foot sliding, 6-foot plug). These, lettered ABOX (single-door cars were RBOX), **16**, began arriving in 1978 and eventually totaled about 2,400 cars.

The recession and traffic downturn of the 1980s led Railbox to sell about 11,000 cars to individual railroads in the 1980s and later. Some of these were repainted and relettered, but many were merely restenciled with the new owners' reporting marks.

Many Railbox cars remain in service in the late 2010s. Many have been repainted in a simplified scheme starting in the mid-1990s. These, **15**, use a paler yellow color, thinner lettering, and smaller arrow logo compared to the as-built scheme.

Incentive-per-diem (IPD) boxcars

To spur construction of additional new boxcars, in the early 1970s the ICC approved a higher per diem rate (the

| Stanray Dreadnaught | Stanray split-corrugation | Pullman-Standard | Non-terminating |

Ends

Boxcar ends were dominated by the improved Dreadnaught end (from Standard Railway Equipment Co., or Stanray). These featured a series of horizontal corrugations that tapered at each end, with narrow corrugations between them. The ends are in multiple sections riveted or welded together, and the basic way to identify the size of the end was by the number of corrugations on the top and bottom section. A rare Stanray variation was what it called the high-capacity Dreadnaught end, which had distinctive split corrugations (the corrugations in an X pattern).

Pullman-Standard used a proprietary end that had a series of broad corrugations that didn't narrow at the ends as the Dreadnaughts did. Along with Pullman's own cars, these ends were used by some railroads and other builders as well.

In the 1970s, non-terminating ends became common. On these, the sides continued past the ends, with the ends featuring horizontal corrugations. These corrugations varied in shape and width; Pullman offered a version with narrower corrugations.

Pullman-Standard's 5,344-cf car was popular among short lines and Class I railroads. It has a flat roof that wraps around the tops of the sides and P-S-style non-terminating ends. *R.J. Wilhelm; J. David Ingles collection*

Pullman-Standard and others made "waffle-side" cars. The corrugations provided interior space for load-restraint anchors. This car, built for Rock Island in 1973, has a peaked roof and 10-foot P-S doors. *Jeff Wilson*

daily fee a railroad paid the car-owning railroad when a car was online) for new railroad-owned cars, making them an appealing financial option as opposed to rebuilding older cars. This led to the incentive-per-diem (IPD) boxcar.

Seeing a chance to make money on this, several investment companies entered the boxcar business by buying large fleets of new cars and operating them through short-line railroads. Major investment groups included National Railway Utilization Corporation (NRUC), Itel (formerly SSI), Emons, Brae, and Trans Union. Their logos would sometimes appear on the cars they financed.

The groups' investment in these IPD cars provided a better return than by straight leasing of the cars as private owners (because of the per-diem payment as opposed to a mileage charge and lease rate).

To make sure they ran loaded as much as possible, the owners classified the IPD cars as free-runners. The result was that dozens of short lines acquired about 30,000 boxcars from 1974 through 1980. Most wore bright, colorful paint schemes. For many of these railroads, the boxcars they owned would more than fill the mileage of the line owning them.

And, although IPD cars get a lot of attention, Class I railroads also acquired boxcars during this period as well.

Although built by several manufacturers with varying features, the boxcars built during this period

followed similar designs. Like Railbox cars, almost all were 70-ton, 50-foot cars, with Plate B or C clearance. Most were external-post design with single 10-foot sliding doors, but some had double-doors (two 8-foot doors for a 16-foot opening). Most had end-of-car cushioning with 10" travel.

There are too many builders and variations to include examples of all, but variations include the type of end, roof, and door, along with the style of side sills, ladders, grab irons, and other details. Many builders changed features or offered multiple options during production.

Among the most common cars of this period was the Pullman-Standard 5,344-cubic-foot car, **17**. It is a Plate C car with non-terminating ends with small corrugations, flat roof that

wraps over the tops of the sides and posts, long straight side sills with an angled notch at the corner stirrups, and 10 posts on each side. Most had Youngstown doors, but some had P-S doors.

The P-S 5,277-cf car was mainly built for Railbox, **15**. Pullman also offered a car with a peaked roof, tighter post spacing (12 per side), and horizontal protrusions between posts. These were known as "waffle-side" cars, and came in several patterns, **18**. The corrugations provided recessed spaces in the interior for mounting load-anchoring devices.

The common FMC design was a 5,077-cf car with non-terminating ends with broad corrugations, peaked roof, and 12 posts per side. The side sill steps down slightly under the second

Doors

Boxcar doors fall into two basic categories: sliding and plug. Sliding doors are less expensive, but they can allow dust and grime to enter a car. Plug doors fit into the opening, providing a much tighter seal. They are also more expensive and require more maintenance.

Plug doors are used on all insulated boxcars and refrigerator cars (see Chapter 9). They also became popular on other cars where lading protection was especially important, especially cars carrying auto parts, food products, and paper. They vary by pattern (number of panels) as well as style and shape of their locking bars and levers.

The most common sliding door is the Youngstown (**2**, **14**, **17**), with multiple horizontal corrugations in a variety of patterns. Superior doors (**8**, **22**, **26**) have a series of horizontal panels. The panels can vary in number and width.

Pullman-Standard had its own design (**15**, **18**), although buyers of P-S cars could specify other doors as well. They had four corrugations per panel, one corrugation of which was shorter than the others. Early P-S doors looked like Superior doors, but with raised panels.

ACF built this Apalachicola Northern 5,300-cf Plate C car in 1977. It has a double-tapered side sill and Youngstown door. These cars were financed by SSI. *R.J. Wilhelm; J. David Ingles collection*

This Plate B car was built by Berwick in 1978. Note the tapered side sill, narrow-corrugation non-terminating end, X-panel peaked roof, and wheel-ratchet door opener. *R.J. Wilhelm; J. David Ingles collection*

This Pickens car is from the first order of Evans/USRE cars, built in March 1977. It has a diagonal-panel roof, Dreadnaught ends, and straight C-channel side sill between bolsters. *R.J. Wilhelm; J. David Ingles collection*

post in from each end, **14** and **16**. The company also had 5277s and 5347s, with the main difference height: the 5077 is a Plate B car and the others are C.

ACF's common IPD cars had non-terminating ends with wide corrugations. These cars had fishbelly-style side sills that stepped down twice at each end, much like the company's earlier boxcars, **19**.

Berwick's cars built starting in 1972 had non-terminating ends with shallow corrugations, X-panel roofs, and side sills that stepped down. Most common were Plate C cars with a 5,277-cf capacity and Plate B cars with a 5,037-cf capacity, **20**.

Evans built 50-foot X-post boxcars through two of its subsidiary companies, U.S. Railway Equipment (USRE) and Southern Iron & Equipment Co. (SIECO). They shared many characteristics, namely a straight C-channel side sill that ran from bolster to bolster (the channel turned inward), **21**.

Cars could have Dreadnaught or heavy-corrugation non-terminating ends (some USRE cars had Stanray ends with split-corrugation/X-pattern ends) and diagonal-panel or X-panel roofs. Late Evans cars had side sills that extended all the way to the ends of

22

Late Evans/SIECO 50-foot cars had side sills that extended all the way to the ends of the car. This one has 12 side posts; the car in 21 has 14 posts. *R.J. Wilhelm; J. David Ingles collection*

the cars, **22**. These could be purchased assembled or as kits from Evans.

Pacific Car & Foundry built 50-foot cars with 14 side posts, non-terminating ends, and X-pattern roofs, **23**. The car had side sills with a slight downward taper at each truck.

Mexican builder CNCF (Constructora Nacional de Carros de Ferrocarril) also built some IPD cars (and cars for one Class I, Rock Island). Its cars had 12 side posts, straight side sills, and either improved Dreadnaught ends or split-corrugation (or bifurcated) ends.

A prominent feature on many IPD cars (especially those owned by NRUC group railroads) were Hennessey Slidewell wheel-ratchet door openers, **20, 21, 22**. These have a wheel to the right of the door that travels along a horizontal geared bar.

Transition and downturn

During the heyday of the IPD car, Class I railroads were buying cars as well. Some were general-purpose cars; others were specialty cars. Boxcars for newsprint and other paper—shipped in large rolls—often have plug doors, **24**.

23

Pacific Car & Foundry built this Boston & Maine car in 1979. It has a flat X-pattern roof, 14 side posts, and Youngstown doors. The side sills have a small taper. *Trains magazine collection*

This Canadian Pacific car, built by NSC in 1979, is assigned to international newsprint service. It has a plug-door and a smooth interior lining to protect the lading. *R.J. Wilhelm; J. David Ingles collection*

Cars for lumber products often had double doors, **25**. Dimensional lumber traveled in all-door boxcars and would soon be traveling mainly by center beam cars (Chapter 7), but double-door boxcars (standard and high-cube) continue to be used for plywood and other sheet products.

There were also 60-foot general-service (non-auto-parts) cars being built, **26**. These were primarily purchased by Class I railroads.

By 1980, the recession that would shortly drive several car builders out of business was hitting the rail industry hard as traffic levels dropped dramatically. This created a glut of previously "scarce" boxcars. Class I railroads, not wanting to pay the high IPD rate, were using their own cars for the reduced amount of business that remained, sending the IPD cars back to their home rails.

The boxcar boom had crashed, and as cars were returned to their owners, many short lines didn't even have room to store all their cars on their own rails—much less enough on-line customers to keep the cars loaded. Investors could no longer make payments, and many cars were foreclosed upon, stored, and eventually resold to new owners at bargain prices.

The recession and the continuing shift of traffic to other specialized cars led to a dramatic downturn in the number of boxcars in service: from 450,000 in 1977 to 190,000 by 2003. The glut of 50-foot IPD cars, many of which eventually found new homes on Class I lines, regionals, and other short lines, meant that very few new boxcars were built from 1980 through the early 1990s.

Many older IPD and other cars are still in service, and many have been rebuilt.

Double-door cars were often used for lumber products. This 50-foot car has a 16-foot door opening with a pair of 8-foot Youngstown doors. It was built by Pacific Car & Foundry in 1979. *Jeff Wilson*

26

This 60-foot, waffle-side boxcar was built in the early 1970s by FMC. It has a 10-foot Superior door. It has been rebuilt and repainted by BNSF. *Jeff Wilson*

110-ton cars

The trend for new boxcars has been toward 110-ton (286K GRL) cars. As of 2018, about half of all boxcars in service are 286K cars, and all new boxcars delivered since 2001 have been 286K cars.

High-cube cars have become the de facto standard, popular for paper, auto parts, and other types of service, **27**. Along with railroad-owned cars, continuing the Railbox tradition of pool cars are two types of 286K cars managed by TTX with FBOX and

TBOX reporting marks. These began arriving in 2003.

The FBOX, **1**, is a high-cube, 50-foot (Plate F) boxcar with a single 10- or 12-foot plug door on each side. They have been built by NSC, Johnstown America, Gunderson, and

27

Gunderson built this 60-foot (68-foot outside length), excess-height car for Norfolk Southern in 1997. It has two 8-foot plug doors. *Jeff Wilson*

The 60-foot, double-door TBOX cars have been built by three manufacturers. This Gunderson car can be spotted by the slightly wider vertical posts above each truck. *Jeff Wilson*

Trinity. They have exterior posts with horizontal members.

Cars have the same basic design, but there are subtle differences among builders in side sills and jacking pads. The first NSC cars have 10-foot door openings, with 14 side posts; later cars have 12-foot doors and 12 posts.

The TBOX, **28**, is a 60-foot, high-cube Plate F car with double plug doors (16-foot opening) and 15" cushioning. These have been built by NSC, Gunderson, and Trinity. Gunderson cars have a wider post above each truck; Trinity cars have narrower end corrugations with wider spacing than the NSC and Gunderson cars.

Although the overall number of boxcars continues to decline, especially as older 70-ton cars hit their mandatory retirement ages, new boxcars continue to be built, **29**. As long as there are paper, auto parts, plywood, and other commodities to be carried, there will be boxcars to carry them.

This 50-foot, 286K boxcar is typical of modern boxcars. Built in 2018 by Gunderson, the excess-height car has a single plug door and the floor is rated at 70,000 pounds axle loading for fork trucks. *Cody Grivno*

1

CHAPTER FIVE

Coal-service hoppers and gondolas

The hopper car has long been virtually synonymous with the term "coal car." The emergence of unit trains in the 1960s and the advent of rotary dumpers have meant coal being carried in larger cars and traveling in jumbo gondolas as well as hoppers, **1**. This chapter will look at how coal hoppers and gondolas have evolved.

A string of aluminum bathtub gondolas trails Union Pacific locomotives in Nebraska in 2006. The UP's double-track main line across Nebraska hosts many daily unit trains, with Powder River coal heading east and empty cars returning west. *Jeff Wilson*

Offset-side construction, where side sheathing was outside the side posts, was falling out of favor by 1960. This 70-ton, three-bay car was built in 1953; a few such cars were built into 1961. *John Ingles; J. David Ingles collection*

Louisville & Nashville 191070 is one of 775 class H-55, 100-ton, exterior-post cars built in 1964 to this design. The exterior-post, 3-bay car has a 3,407-cf capacity. *John Ingles; J. David Ingles collection*

History and design

Coal cars were among the first steel cars, as well as the first built in large numbers with higher capacity. Coal haulers such as Norfolk & Western and Virginian built 100-ton gondolas as early as the 1910s (and the Virginian had 120-ton, six-axle cars as well). However, these were strictly for on-line use, mainly to get coal from on-line mines to tidewater. Large cars for general service across the country wouldn't arrive until the 1960s.

The standard hopper car through the steam and diesel transition era was the two-bay, 50-ton offset-side car. A three-bay, 70-ton version was growing in popularity by the end of the 1950s, 2. Cars built to American Railway Association (later Association of American Railroads) designs dominated, but some railroads and manufacturers built cars to their own designs as well.

The offset-side design—smooth exterior sides riveted to internal vertical posts—provided a bit more cubic capacity compared to an outside post car of the same dimensions. However, the design was weak, especially with larger cars, as the load pressed against the sides and pushed them away from the posts.

By the 1960s, almost all new 70-ton and larger cars were exterior-post designs, 3, with sides welded or riveted inside of vertical posts. Many offset-side cars were eventually rebuilt with exterior posts in the 1960s.

Small-car traffic began dropping off by the late 1950s. Small-town coal dealers were going out of business as home heating shifted to fuel oil and natural gas (or LPG). There were also fewer small power plants and industrial users as customers for shipments of one or a few cars.

Coal-hauling railroads were still running solid trains from mine areas to ports or large industrial areas, but mine traffic was evolving: The move was toward fewer, but larger, more-efficient mines, and away from multiple small operations that only loaded a few cars per day. Larger cars followed.

The major traffic change came in the 1960s with a dramatic increase in construction of large coal-fired power plants across the country, with coal shipped at first in large blocks of cars and then in unit trains.

Bethlehem built this 100-ton, 4-bay car for Missouri Pacific in 1975. The 51-foot car has a 12'-1" extreme height.
Jeff Wilson

This was an important distinction compared to the solid coal trains then operating, which were large groupings of single-car shipments, often originating at multiple mines, going to common destinations.

By definition, a unit train has all cars traveling under a single waybill to a single customer—for example, 100 cars loaded at one mine and destined for one power plant. Unit trains allow efficiency, as they can travel long distances without en route switching. They could be loaded at large mines with flood loaders, where a train could be loaded while in motion—in one solid block, if a loop track could be used.

By the mid-1960s, 100-ton cars of many hopper and gondola types were coming into wide use, many built specifically for unit-train service. Rotary couplers became common on both hoppers and gondolas, allowing more-efficient unloading by rotary dumpers at utilities.

The opening of huge low-sulfur surface coal mines in Wyoming's Powder River Basin in the 1970s spurred even more carbuilding. These new cars could be owned by either railroads or utilities.

The first private-owner hopper cars for unit train service were Pennsylvania Power & Light's Bethlehem-built hoppers. The 100-ton, 3,366-cf cars were built in 1964. *Trains magazine collection*

Modern hoppers

The move to 100-ton hopper cars was accomplished with different designs among car builders. Many were stretched versions of 70-ton exterior-post cars, with three or four outlet bays, **4**.

Car length and height varied by builder and order, with cubic capacity also varying. Western (sub-bituminous) coal is less dense than eastern (bituminous) coal, so cars designed for western mines are typically slightly larger than eastern cars—around 4,000

cf compared to 3,500 cf. Variations of these cars would be built through the 1980s.

A driving force in car design was the move toward unit train service in the early 1960s. Pennsylvania Power & Light was the first utility to buy its own cars for unit train service. The initial 74 cars were 3,366-cf, 100-ton cars built by Bethlehem in April 1964, **5**. Although the cars were three-bay hoppers, they were designed for dumping in rotary unloaders.

Bethlehem (later Johnstown

This Chicago & North Western rotary car is typical of 100-ton coal hoppers in the unit-train era. The 4,000-cf car was built by Pullman-Standard in 1975. The white panel marks the rotary-coupler end. *Jeff Wilson*

Norfolk & Western built many of its own hopper cars. Class H11B car no. 5625 was built in the railroad's Roanoke, Va., shops in 1966. The 263K GRL car has a light weight of 58,500 pounds. *John Ingles; J. David Ingles collection*

Ortner's Rapid-Discharge coal cars had a distinctive appearance, with five outlet bays and the end slope sheets meeting the roof before the end framing. This 3,850-cf car was built in 1976. *Ortner*

America, now FreightCar America) was and is a dominant maker of coal hoppers, though many cars have been built by Pullman-Standard, **6**, Thrall, Ortner, Greenville, Trinity, and others. Many railroads—especially dominant coal haulers such as Norfolk & Western, **7**, Pennsylvania, and Chesapeake & Ohio, also built large numbers of cars.

In identifying cars, look at the overall height and length, the number and style of vertical posts, the style of the ends and slope sheets, and the number and style of the outlet bays. Riveted construction remained popular, although some hoppers were welded. Aluminum hoppers began appearing in larger numbers in the 1980s.

Ortner began building its Rapid Discharge (RD) cars in the mid-1960s. These had additional bottom outlets (five bays) and were designed to clear loads quickly, **8**. The biggest advantage is that the outlet gates are opened and closed by air and activated by electricity (all at once), so there was no need for a person to open latches by hand. The cars can be unloaded while in motion, with each taking less than 30 seconds to dump its load.

They were made in many sizes for varied lading. Trinity continued to offer this basic design after acquiring Ortner, **9**.

Johnstown America's answer to the Rapid Discharge car was the Autoflood

9

Trinity built this 4,200-cf Rapid Discharge car. The 58-foot car has a height of 13'-0". These were popular with utilities still using bottom-dump instead of rotary unloaders.
Trinity Industries

10

Johnstown America's quick-discharge car was the aluminum-body Autoflood. This 286K (110-ton), 4,300-cf car has rotary couplers and five outlet bays. *Jeff Wilson*

car. The 110-ton aluminum car has a distinctive smooth sides with widely spaced vertical stiffeners above each outlet gate and tall posts at each end, **10**.

Thrall, **11**, also offered a similar aluminum car, but with more-typical vertical-post construction.

Even with the move to specialized gondolas and various aluminum designs, conventional steel hoppers have been built in recent times, as witnessed by the 110-ton, three-bay BNSF car in **12**. The car has a light weight of 61,000 pounds, about 11,000 pounds heavier than the Trinity, Johnstown America, or Thrall aluminum cars.

Spotting features

Check the length of the car, its cubic capacity, and whether the car has rotary couplers. Prominent features are the side construction (smooth sides or exterior posts), and the number, style, and spacing of posts. Construction material (aluminum or steel) and assembly method (riveted or welded) are also identifiers.

For hoppers, also look at the number and style/orientation of outlet bays. For gondolas, look at the body shape: Is it a rectangular box, or does it have end slopes and protruding below-body tubs? Cars designed for rotary-dump, unit-train service (contrasting end) will have a length of 53'-1".

The end framing also varies among designs: Check if the side sill goes straight through the end platform or if it steps down. Look for the size and number of vertical braces at the car ends, how high the slope sheet is where it meets the end, and the style of ladders and grab irons and how they are attached to the bracing.

11

Thrall's five-bay aluminum car featured more-conventional exterior-post construction. This 3,980-cf, rotary-coupler car was built in 1994. *Jeff Wilson*

12

This traditional-style steel hopper was built by FreightCar America in 2007. The 110-ton steel car has riveted construction, three bays, and a rotary coupler.
Jeff Wilson

13

Southern Railway's "silversides" cars were the first aluminum-body coal gondolas. The 100-ton cars were built by Pullman-Standard in 1960.

John Ingles; J. David Ingles collection

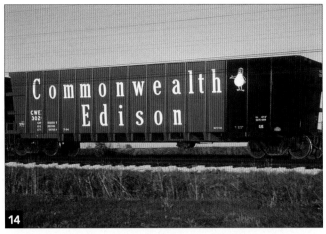

14

Thrall built 4,000-cf steel gondolas for ComEd in 1964, the first unit-train cars with rotary couplers. Thrall's cars had slightly angled sides and ends, with heavy side posts.

John Ingles; J. David Ingles collection

15

Thrall continued building steel gons through the 1970s. This 4,550-cf car, built in 1975, had an experimental hinged roof that would prove extremely impractical.

Thrall

16

This Greenville 100-ton gon, built in 1966, has a 3,700-cf capacity. The common design featured alternating light and heavy posts.

John Ingles; J. David Ingles collection

Coal gondolas

The Southern Railway gets credit for buying the first modern coal gondolas—which also comprised the first large-scale order of modern aluminum cars—with its "silversides" coal gondolas in 1960, **13**. (Southern was also in the midst of buying the first of its "Big John" aluminum covered hoppers at the time as well.)

Southern bought 750 of the 100-ton (251,000-pound GRL) cars, which were built by Pullman-Standard. The only steel components were the cars' center sills, some brake components, and roller-bearing trucks.

The cars were 52 feet long and 11'-7" tall, with a capacity of 3,620 cf. Each car had a light weight of just 47,300 pounds. This was significant, representing about 5 tons less tare weight compared to a contemporary steel coal hopper car. They were very successful in service, with most serving out their 40-year service lives until being retired in 2000.

In spite of the success of these cars, additional large-scale aluminum coal car orders wouldn't come again until the 1980s. Aluminum was much more expensive than steel, and some railroads remained convinced that steel was a better material for railcars.

The era of specialized coal gondolas was, however, here to stay. Thrall built 4,000-cf, 100-ton cars for Commonwealth Edison in July 1964, **14**. The Thrall cars had a 47'-9" inside length, slightly angled ends, and heavy side posts that matched crossbearers under the car. The company would continue building versions of this car through the 1970s, **15**.

The ComEd cars were significant in that they were the first cars with rotary couplers at one end, allowing cars to be dumped without uncoupling. ComEd acquired 273 of these cars, starting the standard of painting one end a contrasting color to indicate the location of the rotary coupler.

Other companies began building coal gons as well. Greenville's car, **16**, had alternating light and heavy vertical posts. The 100-ton car was built in versions from 3,700 to 4,100 cubic feet.

Pullman-Standard's coal gondola was straightforward, with exterior-post sides and a version of the company's distinctive non-terminating end with multiple corrugations, **17**. The posts on the P-S car ended at the bottom of the side instead of wrapping around like the Thrall car.

Although by the 1980s most cars had shifted to bathtub designs (more on those in a bit), some standard coal gons were still being built. Thrall was offering an aluminum version of its car, **18**, with non-terminating vertical ends and external-post sides. The 4,325-cf car shown in the photo was built in 1991.

An important consideration in unit-train operation is car length. Rotary dumpers do their job with cars coupled, so all gondolas and hoppers intended for unit-train rotary-dump service must be a standard length: 53'-1" exterior length (53'-7" coupled length). Any modifications to car capacity must be done via height or other car design within that length.

Bathtub cars

A significant design emerged in 1969 when Canadian Pacific ordered the first so-called "bathtub" coal gondola, which had a long horizontal tub extending down below floor level between the trucks, **19**. The 105-ton cars, built by Hawker Siddeley, allowed more cubic capacity—4,760 cf— compared to a standard-shape gondola. They do not have rotary couplers.

Pullman-Standard's 4,000-cf steel gon has non-terminating ends and lighter posts than Thrall's design. This one is ending its career as many old coal gons did, in scrap-metal service. *Jeff Wilson*

Thrall built this external-post, 4,325-cf aluminum car in 1991. It was built as a 100-ton car, but converted to a 110-car after 1995. *Jeff Wilson*

Canadian Pacific's first bathtub cars are 5 feet longer than most other coal gondolas. They have alternating heavy/light side posts in a 3-3-3-3-3 panel pattern. *Canadian Pacific*

20 The ACF Coalveyor, introduced in 1978, resembles the older Greenville design but with a bathtub between trucks. It has posts in a 2-2-2-2-2 pattern. *ACF Industries*

21 Bathtub cars built by Union Pacific, like this 4,155-cf car, were shorter than the Canadian Pacific design. Note the heavy V bracing on the end and the two-panel middle side section. *Union Pacific*

The CP bodies have tapered sides and ends, six heavy vertical posts with two narrow posts between each (creating a 3-3-3-3-3 panel pattern), and two heavy angled end supports in a V configuration. The cars have a 48'-0" inside length, and with platforms on each end, they are 5'-6" longer (58'-7") than rotary-coupler-equipped cars.

ACF began building its bathtub-style car, the Coalveyor, **20**, in 1978. The car had 11 side posts, with heavy and light posts alternating, and was offered in several sizes (4,240-cf shown). They were built until 1981.

Berwick, Greenville, Thrall, and the Union Pacific, **21**, all built similar-design cars that strongly resembled the CP design. They had the same type of side post arrangement, with heavy and light posts mixed: 15 vertical posts in a 3-3-2-3-3 panel arrangement between heavy ribs. These were built from the late 1970s through the 1980s. These were shorter, conforming to the 53'-1" length for rotary-service cars.

The most successful tub-style coal gondola has been the BethGon Coalporter, **22**, introduced by Bethlehem in 1978 and produced by successors Johnstown America and FreightCar America. The car has twin longitudinal tubs—one on either side of the center sill—between the trucks. The car is distinctive for its ends, which have slope sheets and framing like a conventional hopper car.

Early versions were steel, but aluminum versions soon became popular, especially for western coal, **23**.

Although aluminum cars were more expensive (about 20-25 percent), the lower tare weight (up to 8 tons per car) adds up, especially considering a full unit train of cars.

All builders upgraded their designs as 286K GRL cars, with many built before 1995. Many cars built before the switch to 286K GRL cars in 1995 had bodies built to handle the larger load, and were stenciled "Car structure designed for 286,000 GRL." Qualifying these cars for 286K was usually a matter of adding new trucks (and/or appropriate spring packages) and restenciling the load limit and light weight (see **18**).

In 2002, Johnstown America began delivering an upgraded car as the BethGon II. It has a similar appearance the the earlier BethGon but a lighter tare weight (41,700 pounds) and increased cubic capacity (4,520 cf). FreightCar America also offers the Hybrid Bethgon II, a combination of steel components with aluminum body, with a 47,800-pound light weight.

Trinity also offers a similar car. Its original Aluminator is a 4,400-cf, 286K car that resembles the BethGon, but the troughs are tapered at each end and deeper at the ends than the middle, making them easy to spot, **24**. Later versions were 4,525-cf cars.

Trinity's newer design is a 4,402-cf capacity car, **25**, with straight-bottom troughs. Trinity also offers a larger car (4,793-cf), which has a horizontal strip along the middle of each side,

22 Bethlehem introduced the twin-tub BethGon Coalporter in 1978, and it would become the most-popular coal gondola in service. This 4,000-cf steel version was built in 1982. *Trains magazine collection*

Aluminum BethGons became popular, especially for western coal. This 286K, 4,480-cf aluminum car is a foot taller than the steel car in 22. *Jeff Wilson*

Trinity's Aluminator looks like a Coalporter, but the tubs angle upward toward the middle of the car. *Tom Danneman*

and a smaller (4,125-cf) combination aluminum/stainless car.

Another distinctive design is the Johnstown America Aeroflo, a lightweight (42,000) design introduced in 1989—it was one of the first 286K coal gondolas. The car has a more streamlined appearance than the Bethgon, with smooth side panels and recessed panels at the ends. It was built through the 1990s, **26**.

The Aeroflo vertical seams are pronounced, with rows of vertical rivets centered on each panel. Early cars didn't have cutouts on the end panels below the slope sheets (except for a notch on the bottom of the right-side end panel at the brake gear).

Ownership, paint, and lettering

Railroads themselves owned almost all coal gondolas and hoppers until unit-train traffic began increasing in the mid-1960s. From that period onward, utility companies found it more economical to invest in their own equipment (purchasing or leasing).

Some early paint schemes were bold, with full lettering indicating the utility. Examples were the initial PP&L hoppers, **5**, and the red ComEd cars, **14**. For the most part, however, schemes on unit-train coal cars are dull. Black was common for steel cars, with aluminum cars left unpainted in most cases. Railroad-owned cars often have a simple logo (sometimes with lettering).

Rotary-dump-service gondolas and

hoppers have the end with the rotary coupler painted a contrasting color to indicate the end equipped with a rotary coupler, with additional lettering ("Rotary coupler end").

Other lettering includes capacity in cubic feet and any warnings about

special handling or equipment (such as cars with electrically activated outlet gates). Heat is often used in winter to free frozen clumps of coal. Aluminum cars carry a warning such as "no thaw heat" or "radiant heat only," as they can be damaged by excess heat.

This 2007-built, 4,402-cf aluminum Trinity twin-tub car is similar to the BethGon, but has a different side sill design and grab iron arrangement. *Jeff Wilson*

Johnstown America's Aeroflo has smooth sides and pronounced vertical seams. This 4,720-cf car is a later version with open cutouts on the ends under the slope sheets. *Jeff Wilson*

1

CHAPTER SIX

Gondolas and hopper cars

This 52'-6", 110-ton (286K GRL) Greenbrier gondola features welded construction, 13 side posts, 5'-6" interior height, non-terminating ends, and tapered side sills. It was built in 2018. *Cody Grivno*

Gondola and hopper cars are, as many have noted, the pickup trucks of railroading, **1**. Open hoppers haul almost any bulk product not affected by weather, and gondolas carry bulky items that won't fit in a boxcar. Hoppers and gons are built for general as well as specialized service. Coal cars are covered in Chapter 5; this chapter covers other variations of open-top cars.

The difference between gondolas and hoppers is that hopper cars are designed for carrying bulk commodities and have bays—hoppers—with angled slope sheets directing lading to outlet gates under the car. Hopper cars are defined as "self-clearing," meaning that opening the outlet gates should allow all of the contents to exit the car.

Gondolas have fixed sides and can have fixed or fold-down ("drop") ends.

Almost all modern gondolas have solid floors. Some specialty cars (namely coal and some wood-chip cars) have curved bottoms extending below normal floor level; most gons, however, have flat, solid floors.

History and design

Hoppers were among the first all-steel cars, with that style common by 1900. By World War I, the standard hopper was a 50-ton all-steel car with two bottom outlet bays. Many designs were used, but the most common were United States Railroad Administration (exterior post) and then ARA (American Railway Association; later AAR, Association of American Railways) designs for offset-side and later exterior-post cars.

Railroads specializing in hauling coal (notably Norfolk & Western, Pennsylvania, Chesapeake & Ohio, and Virginian) developed their own designs, some with larger cars (100-ton or higher capacity) for on-line use. Cars of 70-ton capacity became common by the late 1950s.

Specialty hoppers for non-coal use include ore cars, ballast cars, and aggregate cars, with sizes expanding with the move to 100- and then 110-ton cars.

Through the 1950s most gondolas were 50-ton cars, built in two variations: mill and general-service. Mill gons were long (usually 52'-6" or 65'-6"), low (3'-6" to 3'-10" inside height), and many had drop ends.

As their name implies, mill gons are primarily used for steel mill products, including metal beams, pipe, coiled steel, scrap, wire, and other finished mill products. The drop ends enabled them to carry items longer than the car itself (usually with idler flatcars on either side).

General-service (GS) gondolas were shorter, generally 40 to 46 feet, with taller interiors (4'-3" to 4'-10"). They often carried sand and aggregates, and several railroads used them to haul coal and coke, especially in the era before dedicated coal gondolas came into wide use.

Many GS gons had drop bottoms (doors in the floor that opened downward) to enable easier unloading of aggregates and coal. They were not self-clearing, as their flat floors would keep cars from emptying completely. Drop-bottom cars became rare by the modern era.

Modern mill gondolas

By the early 1960s, new gondolas were either 52- (52'-6") or 65- (65'-6") foot mill cars, **2**. The older, shorter GS gons were no longer popular, largely replaced by new large gondolas designed specifically to haul coal (more on those in Chapter 5).

As with other cars, weight limits grew, with 70-ton gondolas common by the late 1950s. Although some 100-ton gondolas were built during the 1960s,

2

Covered gondolas were often used for carrying coiled steel. Thrall built this riveted 70-ton mill gondola in 1962. The 52'-6" car has Dreadnaught ends and tapered side sills. *Thrall*

**This Thrall car was a common design through the 1970s, with welded construction and tapered side sill. The 100-ton, 52'-6"
car was built in 1973.** *Thrall*

**Greenville and Thrall both built gondolas with corrugated sides, with varying side
patterns. This 100-ton Union Pacific car is 65 feet long.** *Jeff Wilson*

**This Trinity-built 110-ton car is carrying a load of scrap metal. The 52'-6" car has a
straight side sill, common for many modern gondolas.** *Jeff Wilson*

**This 52'-6" Gunderson car has straight sills with a slight cutout at the stirrup
steps, and a ladder at the right side (compared to grabs on the Trinity car in 5).
The one-piece cover is clamped in place.** *Jeff Wilson*

they were generally for specialized
service, with 70-ton cars most common
into the 1970s.

From the 1960s onward, Thrall
became a major builder of gondolas,
with its welded design dominating,
3. Other builders included Pullman-
Standard, Greenville, Bethlehem,
Ortner, Evans/SIECO, and Trinity.

Car features varied among orders
as well as builders. Key identifying
characteristics include the number,
style, and pattern of vertical posts.
Posts often appear heavier on 100- and
110-ton cars compared to 70-ton cars.
Some posts are tapered at the bottom,
while others are a consistent thickness.

Post spacing varies: Some cars have
even spacing among posts; others have
narrower or wider spacing among
some posts toward each end. Some
manufacturers use posts of varying
thickness on a single car, alternating
along the side.

Look at the bottoms of the sides.
Some have straight side sills across
the length of the body, and some
have a slight drop between the
trucks (sometimes called a "fishbelly"
appearance). The angle and depth of
the taper can vary.

Corrugated side panels appeared
on some cars (namely Thrall and
Greenville) in the 1970s and 1980s, **4**.
The corrugations vary in the number
per panel, as well as the number and
location of panels with corrugations.

Car ends also vary. Some cars have
standard Dreadnaught wraparound
ends, with three, four, or five horizontal
corrugations depending upon car
height. Others have non-terminating

Railgon was created in 1979 to provide a pool of 100-ton, 52-foot mill gondolas. This one was built by Bethlehem in 1980. *Jeff Wilson*

Spotting features

For gondolas and hoppers alike, check the length, height, number/spacing of vertical posts, and whether a car is welded or riveted (or combination). On gondolas, look at the type of ladder or grab irons, the side sills (straight or angled), and end design (and whether it has drop ends). For hoppers, look at the cubic capacity, number and style of bottom outlet bays and gates, and the end style (bracing, angle of slope sheets, where the slope sheet meets the end, whether the area under the slope sheets is open).

Railgon added to its fleet with 66-foot, 110-ton cars beginning in 2005. This Trinity car was built in 2007. Cars have straight sills; post design varies among manufacturers. *Cody Grivno*

ends, where the sides extend past the ends, with heavy cross ribs on the ends. Pullman-Standard cars have a version of that company's proprietary ends.

A distinctive design was built by SIECO (Southern Iron and Equipment Co.) starting in 1975. Since SIECO was shortly after acquired by Evans, the 52'-6", all-welded cars become known simply as Evans gondolas. They featured 12 side posts, 4'-6" interiors (except for some 5'-0" cars for C&NW), and straight side sills. They also had a distinctive horizontal line between the side and side sill, with the posts passing over it, with the posts terminating above the bottom of the side sill.

Once the 286,000-pound GRL was adopted in 1995, most new gondolas were built to that limit. The biggest visible change is that new gondolas tend to be taller (5'-6" to 6'-0" interior

height), **5**. They can have straight or tapered sides, **1**.

Some gondolas are specially equipped to carry specific products, usually in assigned or dedicated service. The most common are cars carrying coiled steel, which have V-shaped cradles on the floor. These cars are usually covered, **2**. Although these were largely superseded by dedicated coil cars starting in the mid-1960s (more on those in a bit), many continued to be built, and you can still find them in service.

Other gondolas are also equipped with covers, including those carrying contaminated soil, garbage, or other waste, **6**. Steel covers were once common, but lighter-weight fiberglass or composite shells are now typical.

Railgon cars

Railgon was created in 1979 to provide a pool of free-running gondolas available to any railroad—just like Railbox for boxcars, **7**. A total of 4,000 cars were built in 1980 and 1981.

The cars, all with GONX reporting marks, followed a common design. All were 52-foot cars, 100-ton capacity, with 13 vertical posts and straight side sills. They were built by five builders: Thrall, Berwick, Greenville, Bethlehem, and Pullman-Standard.

After just a few years, a recession and a glut in the market meant they were being underutilized, and many were sold to individual railroads. Most new owners simply restenciled their reporting marks over the originals and didn't repaint the cars.

Starting in 2005, TTX acquired new Railgon cars, this time 66-foot, 110-ton cars built initially by NSC and Trinity, **8**. The cars vary in appearance: The NSC cars are distinctive, with alternating straight and angled side posts.

Coil-steel cars

Conventional mill gondolas fitted with V-shaped troughs (usually with removable covers) were the typical method of carrying rolls of coiled

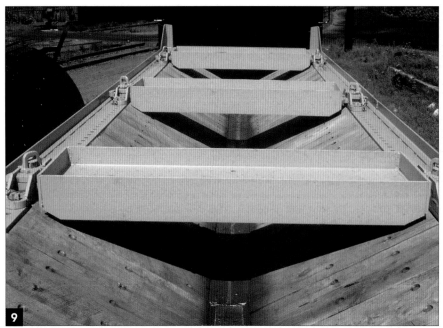

9

Coil cars have a V-shaped trough, lined with wood (or other non-damaging liner) to cradle the coils. The dividers could be locked at any point along the car.

John Ingles; J. David Ingles collection

10

This is a Type 1 Evans coil car, built in 1965. It lacks the side running boards of later cars. The hoods often got swapped among early cars.

John Ingles; J. David Ingles collection

sheet metal into the 1960s. This wasn't extremely efficient, as those steel gondola sides represented a lot of extra weight for its load. Most were 70-ton cars, and coils maxed out the weight limit with space to spare. Also, most gondolas did not have cushion underframes, which helped protect the easily-damaged coils.

The solution was a dedicated car without the tall sides, and with a trough that could be part of a car's structure for strength. Cushion underframes and coil dividers protected the coils from shifting, **9**. Evans was the first to build one, introducing a 100-ton coil car in 1964.

The Evans car had an inside length of 45'-6", dropped side sills, and a pair of removable hoods, **10**. The car was lighter than a typical specially equipped gondola, but could carry significantly more payload. The car type would prove to be extremely popular.

Coil cars carry an AAR classification as gondolas (usually GBSR, with the "S" indicating special loading equipment for a specific commodity and "R" indicating a removable roof). Early coil cars were classified as flatcars (often "FMS"), but regardless of designation, are the same car type.

Evans built cars through the 1970s, continually revising its original design. The length was stretched to 48 feet (Type 2), then side running boards were added in 1967 (Type 3). The most common were Type 4 cars, built from

11

The Evans Type 4 was the most-common early coil car, built starting in 1968. It has straight sides, side running boards, and a 48-foot inside length. *Jeff Wilson*

1968 onward. These had a straight side sill, **11**.

Evans also built several 125-ton versions of these cars in 1966-1967, with most (250) going to Pittsburgh & Lake Erie. Most of these—among the earliest heavy-capacity modern cars—were built to Evans' Type 1 and 2 designs, but were longer (53'-4" inside length).

Other companies were soon making their versions of cars as well, including Thrall and FMC. In identifying them, look for the shape of the side sill, depth of the sides, the presence of any side posts or braces, whether the ends of the bolsters are visible, and the appearance of the ends.

The covers or hoods came in a variety of styles, including rounded, angled, and corrugated. Early hoods were steel; fiberglass and insulated aluminum are now common. Mills and customers always seem to have a difficult time getting matching hoods back on their proper cars, so it became typical for cars more than a few years old to have hoods mismatched in both style and road name, **10**.

A distinctive modern design is Thrall's CoilShield car, **12**. Built starting in 1992, they were among the first 286K coil cars. They feature a well-style design with coils resting in a 42-foot-long trough between the trucks, with a one-piece insulated cover.

Other companies have built 110-ton cars, including Johnstown America (now FreightCar America), with deep, slightly stepped sides with vertical braces, **13**; NSC, marked by deep fishbelly sides, **14**; Thrall's standard design, with slightly stepped sides but no vertical posts or braces, and Trinity, which continued the Thrall design after acquiring the company, **15**. The trend has been toward one-piece shields covering the entire car in lieu of two shields as on earlier cars.

Wood chip cars

Wood chips, a byproduct of the lumber and timber industry, are used to make paper and various wood products. Wood chips are relatively light, meaning it takes a large quantity of them to hit a freight car's weight limit.

Thrall's 110-ton CoilShield began appearing on Conrail in 1992. It's built in well-car fashion, with the cradle below deck level between the trucks. It has a one-piece cover. *Jeff Wilson*

Johnstown America's 110-ton coil car has a channel side sill with vertical members along the channel (doubled at the bolsters) and an additional member between the trucks. *Jeff Wilson*

Coil cars from NSC can be easily spotted by the deep fishbelly style side frames. This 110-ton car has a single-piece rounded, insulated cover. *Cody Grivno*

Trinity followed Thrall's 110-ton design with a channel side that steps down slightly between trucks. The car has a one-piece hood and 42-foot trough. *Cody Grivno*

16

Ortner built this six-bay, 100-ton, 7,000-cf capacity wood chip hopper for Louisville & Nashville in 1963. The car dwarfs the two-bay coal hopper at right. *Louisville & Nashville*

17

This Thrall 6,000-cf wood chip car, built in 1969, has prominent vertical braces that wrap under the body. Hooks atop each side hold the mesh cover in place. *John Ingles; J. David Ingles collection*

18

This FMC 6,810-cf car was built in 1972. It has a distinctive pattern of vertical and horizontal braces. The former Burlington Northern car was acquired by Montana Rail Link. *Jeff Wilson*

19

This truss-style braced car was built by Gunderson in 1966. The 100-ton car has a 6,048-cf capacity. *Jeff Wilson*

Early wood chip cars were often old converted open hopper or gondola cars, often with extended sides and ends. Some railroads rebuilt old boxcars by removing the roofs and extending the sides.

The 1960s saw the introduction of specialized gondolas and hoppers designed specifically for wood chips. These cars were primarily purchased by railroads in timber country, namely the Pacific Northwest and Southeast.

The style of car—hopper or gondola—depends largely upon the facilities of the end user, and whether they prefer bottom dumping (hoppers), rotary dumping, or end dumping (both gondolas). Hoppers tend to be more common in the east, with gondolas in the west and northwest.

Large-capacity (usually 7,000-cf and larger) hoppers, **16**, have been built by Ortner, Magor, Greenville, and others. These vary in overall length, number of outlet bays, and number/pattern of side posts. Some have raised-pattern panels between the vertical side posts. Owners include Norfolk Southern and CSX (and predecessors Southern, Seaboard Coast Line, Chesapeake & Ohio, Louisville & Nashville, and others), as well as private owners.

Large 65-foot gondolas (usually with one or two end doors) became the preferred style of wood-chip car in the Northwest, owned mainly by Burlington Northern (and predecessors), Montana Rail Link, Southern Pacific, and Union Pacific.

20

National Steel Car built this 100-ton ore car for Canadian National in 1965. The load lines indicate full levels for different types of ore. *John Ingles; J. David Ingles collection*

21

Pacific Car & Foundry built this 1,600-cf, 100-ton ore car for Burlington Northern in 1981. Its exterior-post construction is similar to an aggregate hopper. *Trains magazine collection*

These, built by Thrall, FMC, and Gunderson, are unloaded either by rotary dumping or by end dumping on a ramp. Most are around 6,000- to 6,800-cf capacity.

Gondola-style chip cars come in a few basic car types. Thrall and others built cars with heavy vertical side posts that wrap around the underside of the body, **17**. A similar style, built by Gunderson and FMC, features shallower vertical posts with multiple horizontal cross pieces between the verticals, **18**.

Yet another style uses angled pieces between the verticals, resembling a truss bridge, **19**. Cars have also been built with vertical posts only and with smooth sides (interior braces) by FMC, NSC, and Pacific Car & Foundry.

Gunderson in 1965 built 120 composite-side cars with the truss-style framing (50 for GN and 70 for SP&S). These cars used ¾" plywood for sides instead of steel—definitely unusual for this time period.

The latest wood chip cars are bathtub-style cars from FreightCar America that are based on the company's BethGon coal cars. The largest of these 110-ton cars is 75 feet long and 16'-1" tall with an 8,200-cf capacity.

Ore cars

Iron ore—whether raw ore or processed pellets—is a very dense, heavy product. Cars designed for ore service are short, with their length often dictated by unloading pockets at lakeside ore docks.

22

Canadian National began receiving new ore cars in 2010. This 70-ton car, built by ARI, has rapid-discharge gates. *Cody Grivno*

Major ore car operators acquired large fleets of 70-ton cars through the 1950s. The largest fleet was owned by Duluth, Missabe & Iron Range; other major owners included Chicago & North Western, Great Northern, Pennsylvania, and Burlington Northern predecessors Northern Pacific and Great Northern.

As ore traffic decreased in following decades, few new ore cars were built, with many of these early cars rebuilt and remaining in operation through the 1990s and into the 2000s. These cars had cubic capacities around 1,100 to 1,200 cubic feet.

Rebuilding variations included the additions of side extensions to carry lighter-weight taconite pellets starting in the 1960s. The DM&IR rebuilt many of their cars into "mini-quads," with four cars connected by drawbars to form a single car.

Canadian National received some new 100-ton cars in 1965, **20**. The 2,300-cf cars have load limit indicating lines on the outside for both raw ore and for pellets.

Burlington Northern acquired 800 new 100-ton ore cars in the late 1970s and early 1980s for taconite service, **21**. The cars, built by Pacific Car & Foundry and Johnstown America, look much like a shortened version of a contemporary coal or aggregate hopper, with external posts and longitudinal hopper gates.

CN, which absorbed DM&IR in 2011, received new 70-ton cars starting in 2009. These have the same basic appearance of the older Minnesota style car, but with rapid-discharge gates, **22**.

Aggregate cars

As coal hoppers increased in size, shippers still needed smaller cars for carrying more-dense products, mainly

Aggregates are heavier than coal, so the hoppers are typically smaller. This 100-ton, two-bay Bethlehem car from 1972 has a 2,265-cf capacity. *Missouri Pacific*

Ortner's boxy Rapid-Discharge aggregate cars have platforms at each end. This 2,300-cf car was built in 1972. *Ronald A. Plazzo; J. David Ingles collection*

aggregates (gravel, limestone, crushed rock, ballast, etc.). Two-bay cars with cubic capacities from about 2,100 to 2,500 cf became popular for this, **23**.

Like other hoppers, modern aggregate cars typically have exterior-post construction. Most were rated at 100 tons (263K GRL), with a bump to 286K in the mid-1990s. Many look like smaller versions of larger coal hoppers.

A distinctive design was introduced in the 1970s by Ortner, known for its Rapid-Discharge hoppers of various types. The Ortner aggregate car has a squared-off body (with internal end slope sheets) with open platforms at each end—the body itself ends at the bolster, **24**. Trinity, which acquired Ortner in 1984, still has a similar design in its catalog, as do FreightCar America and several other builders.

Ballast cars

Ballast cars are basically aggregate cars with bottom outlet gates that can dump outside the rails, inside the rails, or both. Like aggregate cars, they are smaller than coal hoppers, since ballast is a heavier, denser product. They are used in maintenance-of-way service, both in hauling ballast from quarries to storage areas and for applying the ballast to track. Ballast cars follow the same basic designs as hopper cars, with exterior-post construction standard.

Most hopper car builders have offered ballast cars, as well as small manufacturers such as Kasgro. Johnstown America's 286K ballast car, **25**, follows a style similar to the company's other hopper cars.

Ballast cars have longitudinal bays that allow dumping between rails, outside rails, or both. This 110-ton Johnstown America car, built in 1994, has a 2,652-cf capacity. *Cody Grivno*

Side-dump cars, like this one from Difco, use a pair of air cylinders on each side. They're mainly used in maintenance-of-way service. *Penn Central*

Side-dump cars

Side-dump cars are mainly used in maintenance-of-way service hauling aggregate and ballast, **26**. These cars have a pair of large air cylinders on either side that tip the body while the low side tilts outward, allowing the load to dump very quickly to the side of the track. Cars with 40- and 50-cubic-yard bodies were most common.

Difco (now built by JK-CO) has been the dominant builder, and Georgetown Rail Equipment still builds them.

1

Flatcars, center-beams, and auto racks

Flatcars have long been used to carry heavy, bulky items that don't require the load-restraining guides of a gondola, including machinery, lumber, pipe, boilers, tanks, structural steel, transformers, and tractors. Modern flatcars have evolved into many specialized car types for carrying lumber, automobile racks, and other products, **1**.

A 110-ton Gunderson car carries a load of steel beams in 2006. The 68-foot-long car has straight sides, fishbelly center sill, bulkheads featuring steel vertical members with horizontal planks, and 16 evenly spaced stake pockets along the side. *Jeff Wilson*

This General Steel Castings 53'-6" flatcar is a solid casting and can be spotted by its multi-taper side. The 1964-built, 70-ton Union Pacific car has end-of-car cushioning. *Union Pacific*

General-purpose cars

Flatcars are AAR class F, with subclasses including FM (general-service), FB (bulkhead cars;), FBC (center-beam cars), FA (auto racks), FC (piggyback cars, covered in Chapter 8), and FD (depressed-center flats).

General-service flatcars by the transition era were predominantly 53'-6"-long, with 50-ton capacity common and 70-ton cars appearing by the 1960s. Most followed one of three plans the Association of American Railroads (AAR) had recommended in 1941. Most were riveted, with fishbelly sides that angled downward between the trucks. Decks were wood, with stake pockets along each side.

A common car of this period, built into the 1970s, was the General Steel Castings flatcar, **2**. These were made in 53'-6" (following the third AAR design, which was based on a Pennsylvania car) and 60-foot lengths, with the shorter version more common.

Their bodies were solid castings. Buyers could purchase an assembled car, or buy the casting only, adding a deck, trucks, and brake gear. They can be spotted by the lack of rivets, the double-taper of the sides, and stake pockets that were cast integral with the car.

In the 1960s, manufacturers began offering their own designs. Most opted for a straight side, **3**. These have a heavier center sill, which is often visible below the car in a fishbelly-style taper. These cars are designed to have decks as low as possible for clearance, so the side sills overhang the trucks, covering the top part of them.

Along with individual railroad owners, TTX began acquiring a substantial fleet of general-service and bulkhead flats by the 1970s, **4**. These have been built to common designs by Bethlehem, Gunderson, **1**, Thrall, NSC, and others.

The move to 286,000-pound GRL cars in 1995 was followed by most manufacturers, **5**, with TTX acquiring the cars as well.

Bulkheads come in a variety of heights and designs. Most have vertical posts behind the bulkhead itself, and the side of the bulkhead may extend ahead of the bulkhead, **6**. The support posts may be straight or angled. The bulkhead itself may be lined with wood planks, **3**, or may be plain steel, **4, 6**.

Side stakes may be placed in the car's pockets, or may be integral to the car. Integral or built-in stakes are common on cars in dedicated or specialized service.

Most modern flatcars have brake levers instead of brake wheels, mounted

Straight sides were common by the time Thrall built this car in 1969. It's a 70-ton, 59-foot-long car, with 48'-6" between bulkheads. The box on the bulkhead holds tie-down devices. *Thrall*

Bethlehem built this 100-ton bulkhead flat for Trailer Train in 1979. The car is 73 feet long, with a 62-foot deck between the steel-faced bulkheads. *Trailer Train*

on the side at the B end, **5**. Many bulkhead cars have a conventional brake wheel mounted on the rear of the B end bulkhead, **3**, **4**.

Depressed-center flatcars are designed for extremely heavy loads, **7**. The low deck, which drops down between the trucks, allows as much vertical clearance as possible. These cars are built in a variety of sizes, and typically carry items such as electric transformers, boilers, and tanks. Many have two or three trucks at each end to spread weight. The car in the photo has a capacity of 340 tons.

Center-beam cars

Finished lumber products have always been an important traffic source, but a challenge for railroads to carry. In the steam era, lumber was often loaded board-by-board fashion into standard boxcars—a very labor-intensive method.

Another method was loading lumber in stacks on standard flatcars. This was easier, but still done board-by-board. It also exposed the load to weather, and lumber loads were prone to shifting, especially when subjected to strong slack action or hard coupling.

The 1960s saw the development of bundled lumber loads, which could be easily handled by forklifts and could be packaged/covered to withstand weather. These were typically loaded on bulkhead cars—a great improvement, but securing the loads was still challenging.

Another potential solution was the all-door boxcar (see Chapter 4). These offered excellent protection and provided a secure environment, but they were complex, expensive, high-maintenance cars.

The ultimate solution proved to be the center-beam flatcar (AAR class FBC). The car is a bulkhead flat with a center wall or girder to which bundled loads can be secured. Canadian National first developed the idea, licensing the design to Thrall in 1969. It took another eight years for the idea to really take off.

In 1977, Thrall built the first 60-foot (length between bulkheads) center beams of what would become

5

This 65-foot, 110-ton Johnstown America flat is carrying a load of sheet steel. Tie-downs are anchored in the stake pockets. Note the lever-style brake handle on the side at right. *Jeff Wilson*

6

FreightCar America built this 110-ton bulkhead flat in 2013. Its side stanchions fold down when not in use. The 57-foot car has a 52'-8" length between bulkheads. *Cody Grivno*

7

This Trailer Train depressed-center flat has a 685,000-pound capacity. It is 108 feet long with a 32-foot platform. It rides on six 4-wheel trucks and has a light weight of 260,000 pounds. *Cody Grivno*

8

The first production center-beam cars were these "opera-window" cars built in 1977 by Thrall. The first ones had a 60-foot length between bulkheads.

R.J. Wilhelm; J. David Ingles collection

9

Gunderson's initial 60-foot center-beam is similar to the Thrall car, but the openings are a different shape and the end openings are smaller than the others.

Jeff Wilson

10

Gunderson (shown) and Thrall both began offering 73-foot versions of the opera-window design. They were primarily used for untreated lumber. This one was built in 1972.

Jeff Wilson

11

Cables secure the lumber loads, with metal angles protecting the corners. Cables lock into slots on the roof and on vertical posts. The floor beams are set at a slight angle inward. *Jeff Wilson*

a common design for Burlington Northern, Milwaukee Road, Union Pacific, and Western Pacific, **8**. These became known as "opera-window" cars, as the center partition had tall oval holes cut in most panels to save weight.

The center beam or girder is vital to the strength of the car—note the absence of a heavy below-floor center sill. The design allowed a much lighter weight—about 4 or 5 tons less than a conventional bulkhead flatcar. Shippers and customers alike became fans of the cars, as they were easy and quick to load and unload.

Gunderson's initial car resembled the Thrall design, **9**. The main difference is that the holes at each end aren't as tall as the others.

Both companies soon offered 73-foot versions of the car, which would become more popular than the shorter car, **10**. The longer cars are typically used for bundles of finished lumber, while the shorter cars carry denser products such as plasterboard, laminates, and green lumber.

Most of Thrall's long cars had 13 windows (compared to 12 on the 60-footer); Gunderson's early cars had 14. The number varied among orders.

On all cars, the vertical posts along the center beams are angled slightly inward on each side, with the floor (or horizontal beams) also angled to provide a 90-degree angle with the vertical posts. This tilts the load slightly inward, stabilizing it.

Loads are secured by cables that run from winches along the exterior of the

Gunderson built this 73-foot car for Burlington Northern Santa Fe. Note that the end diagonals meet the end bulkheads at about two-thirds of the bulkhead height. *Jeff Wilson*

side up to the top of the beam or to a slot on a vertical post, **11**. Small angles on the cables are positioned at the top corner of the load to keep the cable from cutting into the lumber. Empty cars usually have these cables hooked at angles to the vertical posts. This basic design was used through the 1980s.

Truss-style center beams

In the late 1980s, manufacturers moved to an open truss design with a horizontal top beam, vertical posts, and several diagonal braces. This was just as strong as the earlier design, but lighter—truss cars weigh about 4 to 5 tons less than an opera-window car (for a 73-footer).

Most manufacturers adopted a similar design, including Gunderson, **12**, Trinity, **13**, and NSC, with diagonal braces angling upward toward the middle with the middle two diagonals overlapping in the center panel. The NSC and Trinity cars are nearly identical, with an end diagonal that connects higher on the end than the Gunderson version—all the way up to the beam.

Thrall cars used a different truss pattern, with the diagonals going upward and outward and no overlap in the middle, **14**.

An early 2000s design from FreightCar America is the FleXibeam, what it terms a hybrid center beam car. It has a lower center beam with X-pattern bracing and a longer (81'-6") deck between bulkheads, **15**.

The end diagonals on this Trinity car go all the way up to meet the beam. The Trinity design and NSC car are nearly identical. *Jeff Wilson*

Thrall's truss design has a pair of diagonals extending upward and outward from the center, with several end panels filled in. TTX owns a sizable fleet of center beams. *Jeff Wilson*

The FleXibeam, from FreightCar America, is termed a hybrid center beam. The car has a longer deck—81'-6"—and a lower beam with distinctive X-bracing. *Jeff Wilson*

Open auto racks saved the auto business for railroads. This is an early Whitehead & Kales rack atop a Pullman-Standard Lo-Dek 85-foot flatcar, built in 1961. *John Ingles; J. David Ingles collection*

Side panels were the first solution to problems with theft and vandalism with the open-rack cars. Many converted cars remained in service into the 1980s.
Trains magazine collection

Paragon built this fully enclosed rack in 1984. The bi-level car features the company's distinctive RAVE (Rack Anti-Vandalism Enclosure) doors.
Chessie System

Spotting features

Look for length and construction method (welded, cast, or riveted) and the number of stake pockets. Check the style of the side: is it straight or does it taper down between trucks? Is it a single taper or stepped? Is there a lip or flange at the top or bottom of the side? Also note the location and style of brake wheel or lever. Also note the deck: is it steel or wood planks?

For bulkhead cars, look at the number and style of vertical braces, and whether they're straight or tapered. Check the height of the bulkhead and whether the surface is steel or wood planks.

Auto racks

Railroads by the late 1950s had lost almost all new-auto traffic to trucks. The old method of carrying finished autos in boxcars was simply not efficient. Pioneering work from the St. Louis-San Francisco and Santa Fe led to the development of the open auto-rack car, one of the most successful modern car concepts, **16**.

These cars featured a skeleton rack of two or three decks on steel framework, which was secured atop a long flatcar. For efficiency, Trailer Train and railroads began using the same-design flatcars for auto racks as for piggyback (trailer-on-flatcar service), so although many 85-foot rack cars were built, the 89-foot car and rack became standard by the mid-1960s. The resulting car could carry up to 18 automobiles.

Open racks were made by Whitehead & Kales, Paragon, Dana, Evans, and others. The flatcars were mainly piggyback flats from ACF and Pullman-Standard. Many designs were offered by each builder; look at the style of posts and arrangement of diagonal bracing in spotting these cars.

Tri-level racks are used for most automobiles. Many were built on low-level flatcars, which rode on trucks with 28"-diameter wheels, for routes with clearance issues (especially in the east and northeast), and were known as "eastern cars." Some tri-levels rode on standard flatcars; these became known as "western cars."

Bi-level cars carry pickup trucks (and in modern times, SUVs and minivans), and in open-rack days were sometimes used to carry autos on restricted-clearance routes. Bi-level racks ride on standard flatcars.

These racks were extremely successful, with thousands built by the mid-1960s. They regained traffic for railroads, but their open design led to increasing problems with damage from vandalism (mainly rock throwing) and theft of parts from cars in transit.

The first solution, in 1970, was to begin retrofitting existing rack cars with solid side panels, **17**. New cars were delivered with protective panels. This cut down on vandalism, but there were still problems with theft.

Open racks could be found in diminishing numbers through the 1970s, and retrofitted-rack cars ran well into the 1980s.

Enclosed racks

By the early 1970s, Paragon and W&K were the only companies building racks. Both developed designs for fully enclosed cars, with production versions delivered starting in 1974.

These would become the virtual standard for this car type into the 2000s, **18**.

These cars have vertical posts with multiple perforated metal panels between the posts. The sides terminate at lengthwise roof-support rails, designed to carry a corrugated galvanized roof. Because of height restrictions on eastern railroads, many early versions of these cars were built without roofs, **19**.

By 1975, W&K racks could be spotted by their radial "clamshell" doors, which rotated open around the ends and behind the side ladders, **20**. The notches on the doors, which cleared the ends of the decks, showed whether the car was a bi- or tri-level.

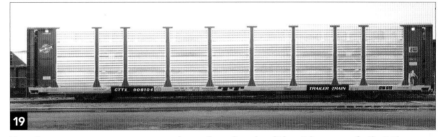

19

For clearance reasons, some early enclosed racks did not have roofs (but they could be added later). This is a 1981-built Whitehead & Kales rack atop a Trailer Train flatcar. *Chicago & North Western*

20

Whitehead & Kales racks can be identified by their clamshell doors that swung open into the notch behind the ladder. This car was built in 1985 and rebuilt in 2006. *Jeff Wilson*

Johnstown America built several hundred distinctive aluminum auto racks for Canadian Pacific and Canadian National in **2004.** *Jeff Wilson*

Thrall's ABL (Articulated Bi-Level) looks much like a conventional auto-rack car, but with a single truck under the articulated joint at middle. *Jeff Wilson*

The articulated Greenbrier AutoMax isn't built on a flatcar, but instead uses a well between trucks to increase capacity. More than 4,000 have been built.
Trains magazine collection

Early Paragon racks had bi- or tri-fold doors, with its RAVE (Rack Anti-Vandalism Enclosure) door appearing as of 1981, **18**. This design was distinctive with multiple vertical slats.

Thrall acquired W&K in 1982, keeping W&K as a division until 1986, then continuing to build the design under the Thrall name. Thrall was in turn acquired by Trinity in 2001. Paragon was acquired by Portec in 1971, which was acquired by Thrall in 1985.

Johnstown America in 2004 built 575 aluminum-sided rack cars for Canadian National and Canadian Pacific, **21**. They have a distinctive appearance that stands out among other rack cars.

The mid-1990s saw a pair of articulated car designs hit the market. Thrall's ABL (Articulated Bi-Level) looks like a conventional rack, but has a single truck in the middle at the articulated joint, **22**. Each body is 70 feet long. The car also introduced Thrall's new Seal-Safe door—the same clamshell design, but without the horizontal notches at the decks.

A more radical design is Greenbrier's AutoMax, introduced in 1999, **23**. These are not built on flatcars but instead have integral well-style bodies, so vehicles on the lower deck are carried below floor level. This allows SUVs to be carried on all decks. They're not in the general auto-rack pool, and are owned by individual railroads and assigned strictly to Honda.

A weakness in car design had been that racks are built as bi- or tri-levels. As markets shift and consumer preferences shift from autos to SUVs, and then back when fuel prices rise, railroads are left with excesses of one type of car. The latest trend in auto racks has thus been to cars that can be converted to bi- or tri-level configuration as needed.

Union Pacific's answer was designing and building a new car, the AutoFlex, starting in 2011. The car can be converted by removing the middle (B) deck, **24**. The most obvious external change was a new door design and the elimination of external ladders for security. The car also included new wheel chocks and other internal upgrades.

Greenbrier followed with its Multi-Max car in 2013, **25**. It can be spotted by the large non-perforated panels inboard from each end. Converting it from tri- to bi-level involves lowering the upper (C) deck and then raising the middle (B) deck directly under the C. Conversion takes about five hours.

Another design is from NSC, which began building convertible cars in 2012, **26**. As with other convertible cars, this one includes a new door design and elimination of end ladders.

All newer rack designs (and rebuilt cars) have panels with fewer perforations, to better limit entry of dust and grime (not to mention spray paint from vandals). Panels now have plates between them as well.

Rack ownership

Historically, Trailer Train has owned most auto-rack flatcars, with railroads owning the racks themselves (although several railroads also operate their own cars with racks). This developed initially as a way to better spread costs among Trailer Train and the railroads.

Most racks since the 1970s operate in a common pool, assigned in groups by manufacturer. These equipment pools are adjusted regularly based on production and need. No effort is made for racks to operate on the railroads that own the specific racks.

Union Pacific designed and built the Autoflex beginning in 2011. The car features a new door design and can be easily converted from a bi-level to a tri-level. *Union Pacific*

Greenbrier's convertible bi/tri-level car is the Multi-Max. It can be spotted by the solid (non-perforated) panels inboard from each end. This one was built in 2014. *Cody Grivno*

This Kansas City Southern-owned rack/flatcar was built by NSC in 2013. Like other new cars, it features panels with fewer perforations and anti-vandalism strips between panels. *Cody Grivno*

1

CHAPTER EIGHT

Well cars, spine cars, and piggyback flats

Several Gunderson-built 53-foot well cars carry J.B. Hunt domestic 53-foot containers near Milwaukee, Wis., in August 2018. Almost all contemporary double-stack cars have either 53- or 40-foot wells. *Cody Grivno*

Intermodal traffic has grown substantially in the past few decades, and now accounts for about 24 percent of total rail revenue, with more than 13 million containers and trailer loads carried annually. As common as it now is to see long trains of loaded double-stack container cars, **1**, it can be easy to forget that well and spine cars date only to the 1980s. Prior to that, long flatcars carried most trailers and containers. Intermodal equipment has evolved significantly in that time.

2

A pair of new 40-foot Burlington Northern trailers ride on a TTX flush-deck piggyback flat in 1978. The flush-deck design became standard in 1968. *R.J. Wilhelm; J. David Ingles collection*

Trailer-on-flatcar—also called TOFC or piggyback—traffic had begun surging in the late 1950s. The formation of Trailer Train Co. in 1955 (see "Trailer Train" on page 86) made interchange movements of piggyback cars much easier, and helped spur railroads to expand service.

The long piggyback flatcar became the standard method of carrying trailers and containers, and remained so into the 1980s, **2**. The evolution of loading and unloading facilities—moving away from drive-on ramps and to lift-on/lift-off straddle cranes and side loaders—led to the development of spine cars and well cars by the 1980s.

Trailer length limits, at 40 feet from the late 1950s through 1981, began growing: to 45 feet in 1981, then 48 feet in 1985 and 53 feet in 1991. The longer trailers made older equipment obsolete. Containers followed trailers in size increases, requiring new and evolving equipment.

Containers grew in popularity while trailer loadings diminished, with rail-based container loadings passing trailers in 1992. The trend continued, and today container traffic comprises more than 90 percent of rail intermodal.

3

This Trailer Train WTTX (Twin-45, retractable hitches, no bridge plates) car is a Bethlehem C-channel design. It's carrying two 45-foot trailers in this early 2000s view. *Jeff Wilson*

Piggyback flatcars

Although 85-foot flatcars were common for piggyback service in the early 1960s, the 89-foot car was adopted as the standard by 1963. Using this length for both auto racks and piggyback service allowed cars to be swapped between these services if needed. Designs were driven by TT—the major buyer of the cars.

Piggyback flats had continuous decks, allowing trailers to be driven on and off at end-loading ramps. Car-mounted bridge plates at each end were folded down to connect cars. Each car had a pair of retractable hitches—middle and end—allowing a pair of trailers to be loaded, facing the same direction.

Piggyback flats were built by several manufacturers. The most common was the Bethlehem car, **3**, which can be spotted by its C-channel side sills, the top of which extended above the

On channel-side cars, the top inside of the channels served as rub rails for trailer wheels. Bethlehem's car had a C-channel, with top and bottom lips facing outward. *Jeff Wilson*

On Pullman-Standard's S-channel cars, the bottom lip faces inward. The hitch is a non-collapsible TT-2 on a KTTX car (Twin-45 car with fixed hitches at each end). *Jeff Wilson*

Trailer Train

The Trailer Train Co.—renamed TTX Co. in 1991—was formed in 1955 with the goal of providing a pool of specialized equipment (piggyback flats initially) for its member railroads. By 1964 this included more than 40 railroads, representing most Class I mileage in the country. Current TTX ownership includes all North American Class I railroads.

TTX is NOT a leasing company. Member railroads pay a reduced per diem and mileage rate, which creates incentives to keep cars moving. Container and piggyback cars comprise most TTX equipment, along with auto racks, other specialized flatcars, boxcars, and gondolas.

Trailer Train has been the major owner of intermodal cars since its formation. Because it is the major purchaser of intermodal equipment, many car designs have been developed by TT (by its mechanical and design committees, which include representatives from member railroads). This means some equipment types are nearly identical, even when built by multiple manufacturers (such as all-purpose flush-deck flatcars and all-purpose spine cars). Other types of equipment vary significantly among manufacturers—well cars, for example.

car side (and served as a rub rail when loading trailers), **4**.

Pullman-Standard's car was similar, but had side sills with an S-shaped cross section, **5**. The top projected outward; the bottom wrapped under the car.

ACF initially made a car similar to the Bethlehem car, but in 1966 switched to a unique design that did away with the channel sides. The car was easy to spot, with multiple exposed cross bearers, **6**.

Another design was General American's G-85 (85-foot) and G-89 (89-foot) cars. Not as common, these relied on a heavy center sill and had retractable trailer hitches that were integral to the center sill.

Low-level versions of these cars were also offered, with 28"-diameter wheels instead of 33" wheels. Although far more common in tri-level auto rack service, this was done on some piggyback cars for operation on restricted-clearance routes, as low-deck cars could be up to 10" lower than a standard car. Trailer Train's had LTTX reporting marks

In 1968, in response to Trailer Train's request for a car that could carry either containers or trailers without modification, manufacturers developed and began building a new flush-deck design. The cars were so named because the deck was level with the tops of the sides, wrapping around smoothly from the deck to the sides, **2**.

Cars equipped for container service had collapsible pedestals built into the deck, **7**. These could be slid along channels and positioned for any length of container. When pedestals weren't being used, they flipped below deck level. Trailer hitches on these cars were collapsible, and when collapsed were low enough to clear loaded containers.

Not all flush-decks were built for combined service; to standardize construction, all cars were built to the same design. Those equipped for both containers and trailers were known as "all-purpose" cars. Trailer Train's received TTAX reporting marks; a smaller number of container-only cars were TTCX. Many railroads bought these cars as well. These were built by

Starting in 1966, ACF's flatcars adopted this design, with exposed cross bearers and lettering on metal plates welded to the ends of the middle cross bearers. *Jeff Wilson*

ACF, P-S, and Bethlehem.

Intermodal service grew rapidly through the 1960s, and by 1965 about 21,000 piggyback flatcars were in service (14,000 owned by Trailer Train). By 1980, TT rostered more than 47,000 of these cars, with thousands more owned by individual railroads.

The move to 45-foot trailers in 1981 prompted changes in car design to allow two of the longer trailers to fit on one flat. This meant either the removal of car-mounted bridge plates to shift the end hitch farther toward the end, **3**, or the use of non-collapsible hitches, limiting the car to lift-on/lift-off service only, **4**, **5**.

As cars were refitted in the 1980s and later, the most common variations became TTWX (all-purpose cars with two 45-footers facing the same direction); KTTX (fixed hitches at each end allowing back-to-back 45-footers), RTTX (fixed end hitches and a retractable middle hitch, allowing back-to-back 45-footers or three 28-footers), and WTTX (retractable hitches, trailers facing same direction, no bridge plates). These were Trailer Train's designations; railroads

All-purpose cars have decks flush with the tops of the sides. Container pedestals slide in a track and can be locked in any position, and fold into the deck when not in use. *Jeff Wilson*

performed similar modifications with their own cars.

Increasing trailer lengths led TTX to create a new type of car by connecting two piggyback flats with a drawbar. Dubbed "Long Runners," the cars began appearing in 1987 and carried TTEX reporting marks, **8**.

They were set up to carry three 48-

to 53-foot trailers by having the middle trailer span the drawbar connection. Early versions built from channel-side cars had their decks widened slightly at the position where the middle trailer's wheels rested; most later versions had a flush-deck car in that position, which didn't require widening.

Trailer Train and railroads have also

To handle 48- and 53-foot trailers, Trailer Train connected pairs of 89-foot cars with drawbars. On these Long Runners, the middle trailer spanned the drawbar joint between cars. *Jeff Wilson*

equipped many other types of flatcars for loading intermodal equipment. A notable group are the 60-foot TT cars that were equipped for containers. Each could carry three 20-footers or a 40- and a 20-footer. They had VTTX and TTCX reporting marks, **9**.

The development of spine and well cars, elimination of end-loading ramps, and the shift from trailers to containers led to the gradual demise of piggyback flats. By 1998 Trailer Train had about 11,000 in service; about 2,000 remained in 2010. Pig flats are quite rare today, with only a couple hundred left on the roster by 2019. Many were rebuilt and re-equipped for auto-rack service.

Spine and skeleton cars
By the mid-1970s, railroads were moving away from end-loading ramps toward larger, more-efficient lift-on/lift-off terminals for intermodal service. A problem with piggyback flats was weight—needing a full deck to support the weight of a trailer and tractor during ramp loading. Eliminating the deck would save a great deal of weight.

The idea of the spine car was to eliminate the deck, making the car as light as possible. The result was a car with a heavy middle center sill, or spine, with a hitch at one end and light platforms to support trailer wheels at the other. Articulating the joints saved additional weight and improved the ride by eliminating slack action.

The first successful car to enter regular service was Santa Fe's Fuel Foiler, a 10-unit articulated car designed for trailers only, **10** (they were also called "Ten Packs"). The railroad tested the car in 1977 with production models coming in 1978.

The car was a success. The cars used 28" wheels, which saved weight and further lowered the profile, eliminating problems with clearance and improving the ride quality. The cars were used strictly on the Santa Fe, but the patents in 1981 went to Itel (later bought by Gunderson).

The result was the Impack (InterModal PACKage) car, along with similar cars from ACF (Versa-Deck II), and Thrall (ARC-5). Variations included the spine shape and profile, the style and shape of the trailer platforms, and brake gear location. Built through the 1980s, these cars were made in 3-, 4-, 5-, 8-, and 10-unit sets, **11**. As Santa Fe had found with its Ten-Packs, the long sets were efficient, but could create problems fitting on terminal tracks and filling out trains. Over time, five-unit sets became most common.

All of these cars were initially designed to carry 40- or 45-foot trailers, and in 1985 they were upgraded to carry 48-footers as well (and older cars were modified). Trailer Train's initial cars wore UTTX reporting marks, later (and modified) cars capable of 48-footers wore TTLX marks.

At the same time as spine cars were emerging, another concept for a skeleton car emerged as the four-unit 4-Runner and stand-alone Front Runner, **12**. Both were owned exclusively by Trailer Train.

The 4-Runner was built by ACF

Trailer Train had about 1,300 60-foot container-only cars in service during the 1990s and early 2000s. This VTTX car is carrying a full load of three 20-foot containers. *Jeff Wilson*

Santa Fe's Ten-Pack Fuel Foiler was the first successful spine car, debuting in 1978. They only carried trailers, and were for Santa Fe on-line use exclusively. *Santa Fe*

This TTLX trailer-only spine car has a different spine shape compared to the original Santa Fe design. Note the heavy fixed hitch and long trailer-wheel platform. *Jeff Wilson*

The Front Runner is a four-wheel skeleton car with fixed trailer hitch and could carry a trailer up to 48 feet (this is a 45-footer). It was an evolution of the earlier four-unit 4-Runner. *Jeff Wilson*

and tested beginning in 1978. It was a skeleton car with each platform riding on four wheels—much like European rolling stock. Four 4-wheel platforms were connected with drawbars to make a single car.

Each platform had a heavy center sill with a fixed hitch at one end and trailer wheel platforms at the other, located below the center sill to improve clearance and lower the center of gravity. Each platform could carry a

40- or 45-foot trailer. Trailer Train received 100 production 4-Runners in 1981 (TTFX reporting marks), but the cars suffered from tracking issues.

The design was altered, and the result in 1983 was the Front Runner: a single-unit, four-wheel car. It was similar to an individual 4-Runner unit, but was longer (allowing up to 48-foot trailers) with different platform, end designs, and wheels. The 4,000 Front Runners (built by four manufacturers)

used either European-style UIC trucks (most) or National Castings Uni-Truck IIs.

They initially received TTUX reporting marks, which were changed to TTOX in the early 1990s during minor rebuilding. Front Runners were more successful—they were handy for filling out consists with single cars where a long spine car wouldn't be filled—but still not popular among railroads. Their light weight caused

13

Container-only spine cars received NTTX reporting marks. They could carry single containers to 48 feet on any platform, or pairs of 20-footers on the end and middle units. *Jeff Wilson*

14

The first all-purpose spine cars could carry trailers or containers up to 48 feet. They had collapsible hitches, with container pedestals projecting outward from the spine. *Jeff Wilson*

issues in train handling and braking, especially if they were placed ahead of other cars. Most 4-Runners were out of service by the late 1990s, with Front Runners gone by the early 2010s.

The last single-purpose spines came in 1987, when Trailer Train purchased 356 container-only spine cars, **13**. These five-unit articulated cars could carry a single 40- to 48-foot container on each platform, and the end and middle units could carry pairs of 20-foot containers. Built by three manufacturers, they wore NTTX reporting marks. Most of these trailer- or container-only spine cars were out of service by the 2010s.

All-purpose spine cars

Container traffic was increasing through the 1980s, and the need for a car that could carry trailers or containers (or any combination thereof) was met by the all-purpose (AP) spine car in 1989, **14**. The AP spine resembles the earlier trailer-only cars, but the hitches are collapsible. Container pedestals are located on arms that extend outward from the spine.

The initial design of these five-unit articulated cars can carry a 28- to 48-foot trailer or 20- to 48-foot container on each platform, and the end units can each carry pairs of 20-foot containers. They ride on 70-ton trucks with 33" wheels (compared to 28" wheels for earlier spines), many of which were reconditioned and salvaged from older cars being retired.

About 3,200 of the original (48-

foot platform) cars were built (TTAX reporting marks), and were used into the 2010s. Several hundred were rebuilt to handle 53-foot trailers and containers from 2004 to 2010.

The design was upgraded in 1993, with the spines stretched to accommodate 53-foot trailers and containers, **15**. The new cars also received TTAX marks, but received "53' All-Purpose Spine Car" lettering. Most were five-unit sets, but some three-unit cars were built. About 3,600 were built, with most still in service as of 2018.

The design was modified again in the late 1990s. Hitches were added to each end of each platform and the wheel decks extended, allowing pairs of 28-foot trailers to be carried back to back. Each platform can carry a single

15

In 1993 the AP spine design was stretched to handle 53-foot trailers and containers. Note the extra "53" stenciling compared to the 48-foot version. *Jeff Wilson*

trailer or container up to 57 feet, **16**. They are lettered "2-28'/1-57' Twin All-Purpose Spine Car" with TTRX marks.

These were three-unit cars, and 2,500 were built from 1997 through 2005. They are likely the last spine cars to be built, as even though manufacturers still list spine cars in their catalogs, the trend toward containers from trailers has shifted car demand to double-stack well cars.

All-purpose spines were built by six manufacturers. Cars were similar, but varied in details, namely hitch

16

The latest spine car is the 2-28/1-57 car, here carrying a load of 53-foot domestic containers. The cars can also carry single long trailers or pairs of 28-foot pups. *Jeff Wilson*

Trailer hitches and container pedestals

Trailer hitches resemble truck tractor fifth wheels mounted on pedestals. They have a mechanism that locks onto the trailer kingpin, securing it to the car. Hitches are of two basic types: fixed and collapsible. Fixed hitches are used on trailer-only flatcars and spine cars that are strictly in lift-on/lift-off service.

Collapsible hitches are used on cars where trailers are driven on and off for loading and unloading, and on combined trailer/container cars where they need to be lowered to allow container loading.

Dozens of hitch models and designs have been used since the 1960s, and hitches can be a good spotting feature in identifying manufacturer and car type. Look at the shape of the horizontal hitch plate, the vertical supports (A-frame or vertical post with diagonal braces), and the style of the supports and bracing.

Containers are secured to each other with inter-box connectors (IBCs), portable devices that rotate to lock in slots at the corner castings of containers. Flatcars and spine cars have pedestals with a pin that can be rotated to lock into the corner casting.

Corner castings are at the corners of 20- and 40-foot containers, and at 40-foot spacing (centered) for longer containers. This allows longer containers to ride on top of shorter ones. International (ISO) containers are 8'-0" wide; domestic containers are 8'-6" wide, but have the slots in their corner castings inset 3" to match the ISO slots.

17

The first production double-stack well cars were built by ACF for Southern Pacific. They were designed for either standard 40-foot international containers or Sea-Land's 35-foot boxes. *Southern Pacific*

18

Thrall's initial well car was the LoPac 2000, licensed from Budd. The five-unit car has all-40-foot wells with a boxy design. Each 40-foot unit has nine side posts. *Jeff Wilson*

design, brake gear location, and wheel-platform design.

Well cars

The increase in international container traffic through the 1970s prompted experiments toward a more-efficient method of carrying containers than on flatcars. The ultimate development was the double-stack or well car, where two containers could be stacked and ride in a depression, or well, that dropped down between the trucks to just a few inches above rail level.

The first such car, Southern Pacific 513300, was built by ACF and began testing in 1977. Railroads had two primary concerns with the car: stability and anchoring the top container. Testing showed that the cars rode well. The initial solution to securing the top container was bulkheads at each end of the car.

The initial stand-alone car was followed by a three-unit test car, then by 42 production five-unit cars in 1981, **17**. These had 40-foot wells and could carry Sea-Land's 35-foot containers or standard international 20- or 40-foot containers. Although successful, they would be ACF's only double-stack cars.

The five-unit articulated car would become the virtual standard length for well cars until the arrival of 53-foot

19

The move to 125-ton cars meant taller sides for the Thrall cars, with wider-spaced posts and a pair of posts in the middle. Note the "125-T" lettering on the end of the well at right. *Jeff Wilson*

The Twin-Stack was Gunderson's first well car, introduced in 1985. It has flat, deep sides and heavy end bulkheads. They are five-unit articulated cars. *Jeff Wilson*

wells in the late 1990s. Several builders soon began building double-stack cars.

Budd was the next company to offer well cars with its LoPac 2000. The design would be licensed to Thrall, which would continue to update the car. The first production cars appeared in 1983, **18**. They were notable in that they did away with bulkheads, instead relying on standard inter-box connectors (IBCs) to hold the top container in place. (Some of these cars were delivered with bulkheads, but they were rare.)

Doing away with bulkheads gave these cars an advantage in that even though they had 40-foot wells they could carry longer (up to 48-foot) containers in the top position. The Thrall cars were boxy, with squared-off wells, a protruding lip around the top of the well, and nine vertical braces or posts along each side.

Thrall updated the design in 1986 as the LoPac II with 45-foot intermediate wells, eventually going to all 45-foot wells and then all 48-foot wells in 1989. The basic appearance remained the same, but with taller sides and 11 posts on the 45- and 48-foot wells. The

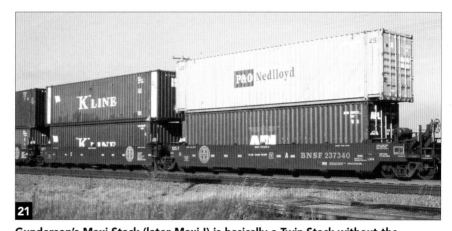

Gunderson's Maxi-Stack (later Maxi I) is basically a Twin-Stack without the bulkheads, with the same smooth-side design. Each well of the five-unit car is 40 feet long. *Jeff Wilson*

increase to 125-ton cars (more on that in a bit) changed the design again, with a pair of closely spaced posts in the middle of each side, **19**.

Gunderson would become the dominant builder of well cars. Its first car was the bulkhead-equipped Twin-Stack in 1985, **20**. By 1988 the company was offering the car without bulkheads as the Maxi-Stack, **21**. This design, with its distinctive flat, smooth sides, became known as the Maxi-Stack I as later designs began

appearing.

To increase well length, Gunderson changed the design by sloping the bottoms of the sides inward. The new Maxi-Stack II had 40-foot end wells and 45-foot intermediate wells, and were only built from late 1988 into early 1989.

In 1989 Gunderson began building the Maxi-Stack III, with all 48-foot wells. The car would become the most common articulated well car, **22**. The sides were slightly taller compared to

Flexi-Van

A notable intermodal innovation was the Flexi-Van, developed in the late 1950s by the New York Central and trailer manufacturer Strick. The system used dedicated flatcars—spine cars with rotating platforms for two containers—to carry containers. The containers were built strictly for Flexi-Van service, and had bogies that were added and removed as they were loaded and unloaded on the flatcars.

Although a few other railroads bought cars and containers, it was mainly an NYC operation, and the railroad had more than 800 cars and 7,000 containers by the mid-1960s. The specialized nature of the equipment and the growth of piggyback and international (ISO) containers kept the system from further development, and it was gone by the early 1970s.

22

The Gunderson Maxi-Stack III, first built in 1989, became the most-popular articulated well car into the 2000s. The design is easy to spot with its beveled-bottom sides and all 48-foot wells. *Jeff Wilson*

23

Trinity's Backpacker entered production in 1987. The initial version had all 40-foot wells. It has beveled sides with a lip at the bottom and angled ends. *Jeff Wilson*

the Maxi-II, but kept the distinctive beveled bottom.

Trinity introduced its well car, the Backpacker, in 1987, **23**. The car, with 40-foot wells, had beveled, smooth sides that weren't as tall as Gunderson's cars. Trinity upgraded it to 48-foot wells, increasing the side height. After acquiring Thrall in 2001, Trinity continued offering the Thrall design instead of its own.

National Steel Car began building well cars for TTX and other U.S. buyers in 1995, **24**. The NSC designs have vertical side posts like the Thrall car, but with rounded openings at the truck cutouts.

Stand-alone and drawbar cars

Gunderson began offering single-unit ("stand-alone") versions of its 48-foot well car in 1991, and other manufacturers soon followed. Railroads found stand-alones handy for filling out consists where an additional articulated set would have empty platforms.

Weight capacity is another advantage: Stand-alones allow any fully loaded combination of containers, whereas multiple fully loaded containers can exceed weight limits for individual platforms on articulated cars.

The Gunderson version was termed the Husky Stack, **25**. Many of these cars had trailer hitches added to the end platforms, allowing them to haul trailers as well (the Husky Stack AP). Drawbar-connected sets soon appeared, in three- and four-unit sets. These

24 National Steel Car's well cars have horizontal posts with distinctive curved ends at the truck openings. This is a five-unit, 125-ton, 40-foot-well car. *Cody Grivno*

25 The Husky Stack AP is Gunderson's stand-alone well car (the AP version has trailer hitches at each end). This is the end unit of a multi-car set connected with drawbars. *Jeff Wilson*

allow heavier loading than articulated cars, with the drawbars limiting slack action compared to individual coupled cars.

Stand-alones have been built in 53-foot versions by NSC (Super Stack), **26**, and Gunderson/Greenbrier. The drop in trailer traffic has led to the removal of hitches from most of the original AP cars.

Longer, then shorter

Well car capacity isn't all about container length—it's also about weight. A fully loaded 20-foot container can weigh as much as a 53-foot container, so railroads have to watch weight limits when loading wells.

Early well cars had 70-ton trucks at the ends with 100-ton trucks at the articulations. By the time well size was increasing, builders began placing 125-ton trucks (with 38" wheels) at the articulations, creating the "125-ton car"—a feature indicated by large "125" lettering on the car sides at the ends (see **23, 24, 28**).

Increasing container size resulted in significant changes to well cars. When 53-foot containers began entering service in 1991, there wasn't an initial need for longer wells, as the 53-footers could ride in the top position above shorter containers on many well car platforms.

However, within a few years 45- and 48-foot domestic containers were quickly disappearing, replaced by the 53-footers. At the same time,

26 NSC calls its stand-alone car the Super Stack. This one is a 53-foot car; it's also found in three- and four-unit drawbar-connected sets. *Jeff Wilson*

27 Thrall built articulated 53-foot well cars before it was absorbed by Trinity. Note the heavy posts at each end and in the middle of each well. *Jeff Wilson*

Trinity's 53-foot double-stack car design resembles Thrall's design, but with angled ends. This is the end well of a three-unit set. *Jeff Wilson*

In 2003, TTX began a program of cutting down many 45- and 48-foot cars to 40 feet, as with this Thrall car. *Cody Grivno*

While some cars were being shortened, TTX was also stretching many older Gunderson cars to 53 feet. The vertical splice welds are visible at each end (bracketing the "53" at right). *Cody Grivno*

international shipping was increasing, continuing with ISO standard 40- and 20-foot boxes. This meant that existing 45- and 48-foot wells were basically obsolete—they were carrying mostly 40-foot containers (or pairs of 20-footers), wasting a lot of space and tare weight.

The first production 53-foot well cars began arriving in 1999, **1**, and TTX had 3,800 of them by 2001. Stand-alone and three-unit (articulated or drawbar-connected) cars are common, with some five-unit versions as well. They've been built by Gunderson/Greenbrier (Maxi-Stack IV are three-unit cars; Maxi V cars are five-unit sets), NSC, **26**, Thrall, **27**, and Trinity, **28**.

To solve the problem of wasted space in well cars with 45- and 48-foot platforms, TTX in 2003 began rebuilding these cars, cutting them down to 40 feet, **29**. Stand-alone cars were also modified. In addition, TTX stretched many Gunderson stand-alones from 48 to 53 feet, **30**.

By 2010, between new and rebuilt cars, the double-stack fleet almost entirely comprises 40- or 53-foot wells.

1

CHAPTER NINE

Refrigerator cars

In an era where other specialty cars have increased in type and number, refrigerator car ownership has dropped substantially. Mechanical reefers now make up less than 1 percent of the national freight car fleet, **1**, with about 8,000 mechanical cars in service—compared to 125,000 combined ice and mechanical cars in service in 1960.

Refrigerator car service has come back a bit in the early 2000s thanks to new cars like this 64-foot (75-foot outside length) TrinCool refrigerator car from Trinity. This ARMN car is owned by Union Pacific, which has the largest modern fleet of reefers. *Jeff Wilson*

Although railroads have recovered some fresh produce traffic, including some unit-train movements, trucks haul the vast majority of it—goods that through the steam era were a mainstay of railroads. The trend toward trucks was well underway by the 1950s and essentially complete by the 1970s. Most existing refrigerator car traffic involves frozen foods, especially potato

products from the Northwest and frozen concentrated orange juice from Florida, along with some produce and wine traffic.

History and design
Ice-bunker refrigerator cars dominated through the 1950s. These were mainly 40-foot, 30- to 50-ton cars that were insulated and had bunkers at each end

to hold ice. Keeping the cars iced was a labor-intensive process. Each car held about 5 to 6 tons of ice, and cars in transit required topping off daily—an extensive operation, as a cross-country trip could take six or seven days.

Cars with mechanical refrigeration equipment began appearing in 1949, but were used primarily for carrying frozen foods—a rapidly growing traffic

Santa Fe built this 70-ton, smooth-side refrigerator car in 1960. The car is 50 feet long (44'-6" interior). The refrigeration equipment is behind the sliding screen door at left. *Santa Fe*

Pacific Car & Foundry built this 57-foot mechanical reefer for Pacific Fruit Express in 1971. It is one of 600 in class R-70-25, the last class of new reefers delivered to PFE. *Jim Hediger*

Pacific Car & Foundry built this 57-foot car for Western Fruit Express in 1965. It has a 9-foot door and is similar to Pacific Fruit Express R-70-14 cars.

John Ingles; J. David Ingles collection

source. Although some ice-bunker cars were "super-insulated," ice cars just couldn't consistently and efficiently produce the sub-zero temps required by frozen goods.

Early mechanical reefers were 40 to 50 feet long, with a compartment at one end holding the refrigeration equipment, **2**. This includes a small diesel engine to drive an alternator, which in turn powers the compressor and fans of a refrigeration unit. A thermostat turns the unit on and off to maintain the desired temperature. An underbody tank or tanks hold the diesel fuel.

The end carrying the refrigeration equipment is apparent, as you'll see a screened (louvered on some early cars) opening on one side and a sliding access door on the other.

Mechanical reefers are AAR class RP (RPL for those with internal load restraints, which would become a majority of these cars). Cushion underframes also became standard equipment on mechanical cars, and most would also be delivered with roller-bearing trucks.

The new mechanical cars worked well, but were expensive—a new mechanical car was two to three times the cost of a new ice-bunker car. The cars' cost could be justified for frozen foods, but not for produce, where the ice-bunker technology—although labor-intensive—worked well and was economical for large volumes of cars.

By 1960, there were about 5,000 mechanical reefers in service—just 4 percent of the 125,000-car national reefer fleet. As the decade progressed, the percentage of mechanical cars rose significantly, but the total number of refrigerator cars also dropped, as ice cars were being retired rapidly (the last ice cars had been built in the mid-1950s).

As produce traffic continued its sharp decline, the cost of maintaining the large icing stations and teams of workers required to keep cars' bunkers supplied could no longer be justified. All icing platforms were closed by 1973, although a few ice cars remained in service in top-ice-vegetable service for a few more years.

5

Fruit Growers Express adopted its white "Solid Cold" scheme in 1982. This 65-foot, 100-ton, smooth-side car was among the last built by FGE, in 1972. *Jeff Wilson collection*

1960s onward

Since the early days of railroading, most refrigerator cars have been controlled by private owners, although most of these were subsidiary companies of railroads. The largest, and the ones that continued buying and operating mechanical cars, were Pacific Fruit Express (PFE, co-owned by Southern Pacific and Union Pacific), Santa Fe Refrigerator Department (SFRD), and the Fruit Growers Express (FGE) consortium—owned by 20 eastern railroads—which also included Burlington Refrigerator Express (BRE) and Western Fruit Express (WFE).

Some railroads owned mechanical reefers outright, including Northern Pacific and Bangor & Aroostook. Other private owners included meat packers, although the number of mechanical cars in meat service was very small.

Mechanical cars by the 1960s were larger than their 40-foot ice-car predecessors, with 57-foot cars common. Pacific Car & Foundry was the dominant builder, providing PFE with most of its mechanical cars, 3, and also building cars for others, including Burlington Northern and its predecessors, 4.

Cars built by PC&F have a common appearance, with welded construction, vertical exterior posts,

6

Union Pacific in the 1990s began rebuilding many older cars, including this 70-ton class R-70-22 car. The bottom of the new end-mounted reefer unit is visible inside the opening. *Jeff Wilson*

wide plug doors, straight side sills, and Dreadnaught ends. Most built during the 1960s had a 57-foot interior length.

Along with operating and owning cars, FGE also built many cars in its own shops, 5. FGE's cars were smooth-sided (sheet-and-post) construction, riveted or welded, with tapered or straight side sills. Cars built from 1960 to 1968 were 55 feet long; later cars were 65-footers.

Pacific Fruit Express acquired the largest fleet of mechanical cars, about 10,000 through 1971. All from 1963 onward were 57-foot, exterior post cars built by PC&F. The biggest changes during production were doors, which

progressed from 8-foot width to 9 feet and then 10'-6".

PFE was split up between owners Union Pacific and Southern Pacific in 1978, with the two railroads dividing the cars. The UP eventually absorbed SP in 1996, re-acquiring many of the cars.

By the 1990s, refrigerator fleets were dwindling and cars were growing older. Union Pacific embarked on an extensive rebuilding program for its aging refrigerator cars, 6. The original refrigeration units were removed and replaced by end-mounted units—which were still concealed in the old equipment area at the end of the car.

7

The ARMN rebuilds included many former Fruit Growers Express cars as well. This 100-ton car is easily spotted by its sheet-and-post construction and tapered side sill. *Jeff Wilson*

8

Santa Fe's largest class of refrigerator cars was Rr-89, 700 cars built in 1966. The 70-ton cars have smooth sides and a 57-foot exterior length (48 feet inside).

John Ingles; J. David Ingles collection

9

This insulated boxcar, built in 1965 by Fruit Growers Express, was assigned to Norfolk & Western. It's 58 feet long (50'-1" inside) with plug doors and straight side sills. *John Ingles; J. David Ingles collection*

This created a distinctive look, with the old screens and access doors removed and the roof removed over the space at the end.

Other upgrades included GPS positioning equipment and remote temperature monitoring. The reconditioned cars were painted white and given ARMN reporting marks. Included in the rebuild program were many former Santa Fe, FGE, and American Refrigerator Transit cars, **7**.

Union Pacific is still the major refrigerator car operator, and many of these rebuilt cars are still operating—and should continue until their 50-year (with rebuilding) lifespans are reached around 2020.

Santa Fe (through SFRD) eventually acquired around 4,500 mechanical cars, building its last one in 1972, **8**. The railroad built many of its own cars, with some built by PC&F. Most were exterior-post cars, 57 and 61 feet long. The Santa Fe got rid of its reefer fleet comparatively early, with most cars off the roster by the late 1980s.

By 1972, there were ample refrigerator cars available for the amount of traffic being handled, and with frozen and refrigerated shipments still in decline, no new cars were needed. Other than rebuilding and repainting the newest of the existing fleet, no new refrigerator cars would be built for more than 25 years.

Insulated boxcars

Advances in insulation materials, namely expanding polyurethane and polystyrene foam, helped revolutionize refrigerator car design in the late 1950s. The new materials allowed a thinner layer of insulation in the walls and roof, while providing much-improved temperature control over earlier materials.

One result was a new car design: the insulated boxcar, classified RB as a "bunkerless refrigerator car," **9**. Most were further classed RBL, with the "L" indicating internal load restraints. By using plug-style doors, an insulated car could maintain temperatures of pre-cooled lading consistently for several days with no need for ice or mechanical refrigeration.

Although more expensive than standard boxcars, insulated cars were much cheaper than new mechanical reefers. Along with carrying perishables that didn't require temperatures near freezing, the cars quickly found use carrying beverages, canned goods, and many other products that needed protection from extreme heat or cold. Many of these products had previously traveled by non-iced ice-bunker cars, but the new insulated cars were more efficient as they provided significantly more interior room (often at a 2-for-1 ratio).

Similar (in some cases identical) cars were given the AAR class of XI (boxcar, insulated). There were exceptions, but through the 1960s if these cars were owned by refrigerator-car operators they were RBL; many railroad-owned cars were XI. The insulated car muddied the waters when it came to determining refrigerator car rosters.

Some early insulated cars were 40-footers, but by the 1960s most were being built to at least 50 feet (inside length). They generally followed contemporary boxcar design, but with plug doors. Through the 1970s many wore the schemes of refrigerator-car operators; after that, they typically wore railroads' standard schemes.

Visible evolutions included a shift from early style smooth doors with V-shaped locking bar controls to exterior-braced doors with horizontal locking bars, **10**. That car represents a common design built by Fruit Growers Express, one of the largest operators of insulated cars.

FGE in 1982 began rebuilding many older cars, giving them new paint schemes: Insulated cars were identified by their familiar "Solid Gold" lettering and yellow paint scheme, **11**, differentiating them from the white "Solid Cold" lettering that began appearing on mechanical cars.

Another common design was a double-plug-door car built by Evans (and its U.S. Railway Equipment subsidiary) from 1969 through 1977, **12**.

As with other boxcar types, production slowed dramatically in

This FGE insulated boxcar has a 10'-6" door and follows typical construction used on FGE refrigerator cars. The 70-ton car was built in 1970. *Jim Hediger*

Fruit Growers Express adopted its "Solid Gold" paint and lettering scheme for insulated boxcars starting in 1982. This 70-ton car has a 50'-1" interior length and 58-foot outside length. *Kenneth R. Combs*

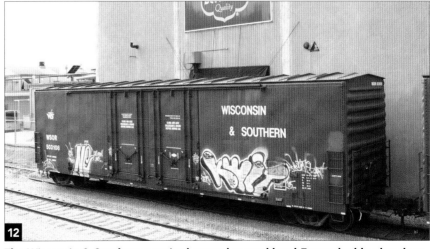

The Wisconsin & Southern acquired several second-hand Evans double-plug door insulated cars. Early Evans cars like this one used Pullman ends. The 70-ton car has a 52'-6" interior length. *Jeff Wilson*

This 100-ton Union Pacific car is an RBL with a 14-foot sliding plug door. It's 59 feet long with a 50'-1" interior length and 10'-4" inside height. *Jeff Wilson*

The first new reefers in more than 25 years were these 83-foot, 110-ton cars from Trinity in 1998. The car has a two-piece fiberglass body atop a steel frame. *Jeff Wilson*

Trinity's TrinCool design has become "the" new standard refrigerator car. They're built in 72-foot versions, such as this BNSF car (82 feet outside) and 64-foot versions. *Jeff Wilson*

the early 1980s with the recession. Many cars built before this period are still in service, with rebuilding or reconditioning common. Although most are 70-ton designs, some are 100-ton cars, **13**.

It can be difficult to spot an insulated car from a plug-door-equipped general-service boxcar. Check the *Official Railway Equipment Register* to make sure.

Modern mechanicals

In 1998, faced with an aging fleet of refrigerator cars but a steady—albeit small—stream of frozen and refrigerated traffic, Union Pacific began acquiring new high-capacity reefers from Trinity, with bodies by DuPont, **14**.

The cars were a radical new car design, with a fiberglass composite body with two-piece (inner and outer shell) construction with a 5" layer of urethane foam insulation between the layers. The smooth-sided bodies are fitted atop a steel frame.

The cars are built to 286K GRL and have a 72-foot inside length (83 feet outside) and are excess height (12'-1" interior). At 7,901 cubic feet, the cars provide almost twice the capacity of older mechanical cars. Other innovations included remote satellite monitoring for both location and temperature, and end-mounted refrigeration units (Thermo-King "Smart Reefer").

These cars led to what has become the most-popular new refrigerator car, Trinity's TrinCool, introduced in 2000 with an order of 700 72-foot cars (82-foot outside length) from Burlington Northern Santa Fe, **15**.

The TrinCool has a more traditional appearance than the earlier fiberglass cars, with vertical side panels visible. The side sills are notched above each truck and at the ladder (non-refrigerator-unit) end of each side. The 286K GRL cars have a capacity of 7,710 cubic feet.

The UP soon placed a large order for 64-foot versions (75-foot outside length) of the TrinCool, acquiring 1,500 of them starting in 2003, **1**. The cars resemble the larger versions

Cryogenic refrigerator cars used a charge of liquid carbon dioxide to keep loads frozen. Early Cryo-Trans cars carried the logos of their lessees. *Jeff Wilson*

and are also excess-height, 110-ton cars with 12-foot-wide doors, but the shorter length drops the capacity to 6,956 cubic feet. They have end-mounted Carrier refrigeration units.

Cryogenic cars

Another modern car appeared in 1990. Cryogenic cars relied on a charge of frozen carbon dioxide to keep their loads cold. These excess-height, 68-foot cars (76 feet outside) were built by Gunderson. The major owner was Cryo-Trans (CRYX reporting marks), with other owners including GATX (which called theirs "Arcticars," and which was involved in a lawsuit over patents with Cryo-Trans), Simplot, and Lamb-Weston, **16**.

Once cars were loaded and sealed, an external connection on the car's A (non-brake) end allowed pressurized liquid CO_2 to be introduced to an insulated storage bunker under the roof. Once inside (and no longer under pressure), the CO_2 changes to vapor and flakes ("snow") at about -100 degrees F.

A 15-ton charge of CO_2 kept a car's interior below zero for two weeks. These cars were for frozen food only (primarily frozen potato products out of the Northwest), as the internal temperature couldn't be regulated as

This 72-foot mechanical refrigerator car was built by Gunderson. The 110-ton, excess-height car has an end-mounted refrigeration unit, standard for modern reefers. *Jeff Wilson*

with a mechanical car.

The 263K GRL cars have a 6,854-cf capacity, and they are excess-height, Plate F cars. They have straight side sills, 10-foot plug doors, flat roofs, and non-terminating ends with wide corrugations.

Advantages to the CO_2 system included the absence of moving parts or mechanical refrigeration units that could break down. A disadvantage was that opening a door would release the CO_2, with no easy way of recharging it. Also, if a car was bad-ordered or excessively delayed, the only way to keep things cold was another expensive

CO_2 charge.

A spike in CO_2 prices by 2000 made cryogenic operation economically unviable. Through 2001, the cars were all converted with end-mounted mechanical refrigeration units added. Most remain in service in the Cryo-Trans fleet.

Cryo-Trans has since added to its fleet a number of new 72-foot (82 feet outside length) cars built by Gunderson/Greenbrier, **17**. These have a 7,780-cf capacity, smooth ends, and end-mounted refrigeration units.

1

CHAPTER TEN

Trucks, brakes, and cushion underframes

Modern freight car trucks, like this 100-ton example, are equipped with roller bearings. At left, automatic knuckle couplers keep cars together, while glad hands at the ends of the air hoses allow a continuous air line throughout the train. *Jeff Wilson*

All freight cars have common components. The wheels and trucks make a car roll, **1**; the brake gear lets it safely stop, and couplers keep a train together. Cushioning devices, found on many cars, work to keep loads safe from slack action and hard coupling. This chapter looks at this equipment.

Wheels and trucks

Freight-car trucks have four wheels: two axles with a wheel on each end, mounted on a frame. This frame, along with springs and other components, is known as a truck. The view in **2** shows the parts of a modern roller-bearing truck. Each truck weighs 4 to 5 tons.

Each car has a bolster at each end—a transverse member across the bottom of the car frame, inset from the end of the body. A kingpin centered on the car's bolster rests in a hole in the center plate at the middle of the truck bolster. The weight of the car body is all that's needed to keep the car on its trucks.

Depending on the truck, the bolster may have pads on each side of the center plate or side bearings atop each sideframe to distribute weight and stabilize the car.

Each end of the truck bolster rests in a notch in the center of the sideframe atop a group of springs (called a spring package). The bolster isn't solidly attached to the sideframe—it's allowed to float up and down on the spring package.

The number and type of springs is based on the weight capacity of the car. Each package usually has seven to nine main coil springs, and each of these springs may have an additional internal spring or hard-rubber or hydraulic snubber. The springs cushion the load and stabilize the ride; snubbers and wedges act like shock absorbers by controlling spring motion, avoiding bouncing and rocking.

Each end of the sideframe rests on the outboard end of the axle. On all modern cars the axle end is a roller bearing, **3**, with a roller bearing adapter on the sideframe. The end caps of the axles rotate, **4**.

Roller-bearing trucks have been required on all new and rebuilt 100-ton cars since 1963, on all new cars since 1968, and on all equipment in interchange service as of 1995. Earlier trucks were solid- or plain-bearing (sometimes referred to as "friction-bearing").

Solid-bearing trucks were maintenance intensive. They relied on brass bearings mounted in the

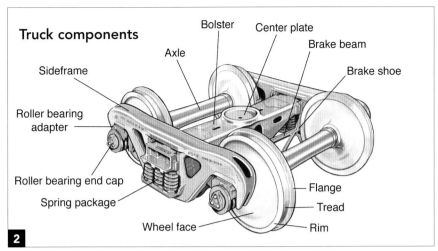

Truck components

Bolster · Center plate · Brake beam · Brake shoe · Axle · Sideframe · Roller bearing adapter · Roller bearing end cap · Spring package · Wheel face · Flange · Tread · Rim

2

Here are the basic components of a modern roller-bearing truck. *ASF Industries*

3

This cutaway view shows the workings of a roller-bearing axle end. The roller-bearing adapter on the truck sits atop the middle section, while the axle rotates on the multiple bearings. *Hyatt*

4

The roller-bearing adapter is often a different color than the truck sideframe. The end caps also vary by builder and type. This is a 6" x 11" bearing on a 70-ton boxcar. *Jeff Wilson*

truck sideframes resting atop the rotating smooth outer axle ends of the wheelsets. These were covered by journal boxes, which contained pads or clumps of stranded cotton (called waste) impregnated with oil to lubricate the bearing and axle surfaces

Journal boxes were checked constantly for oil supply. If a box or bearing ran dry—or if waste or a pad got hung up in the bearing—the result was an overheated bearing, or "hotbox." At best, this meant having to set out the affected car and replace the bearing; if unnoticed, the resulting

fire and heat could result in a failure of the axle, resulting in a wreck. These problems were exacerbated with high speeds or with heavy cars.

Roller bearings are sealed units that require little maintenance—they can go more than 500,000 miles without servicing. They also provide far less rolling resistance and drag compared to solid bearings.

Truck types

Popular modern trucks include the ASF Ride Control, made by ASF-Keystone/Amsted, and the Barber S-2,

from Standard Car Truck Co. Other common trucks include the ASF Ridemaster and National C-1. Each has been made in multiple versions, with 70-, 100-, 110-, and 125-ton capacity.

The best spotting feature is often provided by lettering cast into the sideframe. Also check the shape of the top of the sideframe, the shape of the triangular openings in the sideframe, and the shape and design of the end of the bolster where it's visible through the sideframe.

Brenco is the primary supplier of roller bearings, with Timken, Hyatt, and SKF bearings also in use. Check the color and pattern of the end cap.

Truck capacity is a combination of journal size, wheel (and axle) size, wheelbase, and spring package. Trucks with 70-ton capacity have a 5'-8" wheelbase, 6" x 11" journals (diameter x length), and ride on 33"-diameter wheels. Next up are 100-ton trucks with 36" wheels and 6½" x 12" journals, and 110-ton trucks with 7" x 12" journals.

Wheels

Freight car wheels are steel, shaped to a contour approved by the AAR. A flange on the inside edge keeps the tread on the railhead. Freight car wheels are made in four diameters: 28", 33", 36", and 38". Cars with 100- and 110-ton capacity ride on 36" wheels, while 70-ton cars ride on 33" wheels. Low-profile 70-ton piggyback and auto rack cars use 28" wheels, and the 125-ton trucks used on some intermodal cars use 38" wheels.

Steel wheels are either single- or two-wear. Single-wear wheels are lighter, with a thin (1¼") tread profile, and are designed to be scrapped when the tread (flange/tread profile) wears below a safe limit. Two-wear (or multi-wear) wheels are heavier and have a thicker (2") tread. They can be turned on a lathe and recut to restore the profile to the proper contour.

Two-wear wheels are more expensive, but for heavy-duty or long-life cars they are more economical. The type of wheel used is usually stenciled on the car end (i.e. "1W WROT STEEL WHEELS").

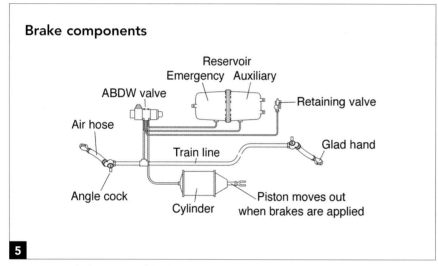

Brake components

5

Every car includes a set of brake equipment, although the specific location of each component varies by car type. *Trains magazine collection*

6

On truck-mounted brakes, the cylinder (just inside the wheel at right) is mounted directly to the bolster. With this arrangement, brake rods and rigging are eliminated. *ABEX Corp.*

Brake equipment

Each car carries a full set of brake equipment. Air brakes have been mandatory since the late 1800s, and the current ABDW system (standard since 1974) is an upgrade of the AB brake system that became mandatory for all new cars as of 1932. The individual components are the same; improved designs have increased reliability and response time.

The drawing in **5** shows how the brake gear components are arranged. Specific locations for each component vary by car: Under the body for flatcars and boxcars, at the end under the slope sheet for hoppers and covered hoppers, and on the end platform or under tank cars. Some cars have truck-mounted brakes, where the cylinder is mounted inside the frame, **6**.

Here's how it all works: The brake pipe, which terminates at each end of the car at a flexible hose with a coupling, forms the train line when connected to other cars. Hose couplings ("glad hands") are connected by hand, with rubber gaskets ensuring a tight seal. They separate automatically when cars are pulled apart.

At the base of each hose is an angle cock, a valve that opens or closes the line. Air compressors on the locomotive charge the train line, generally with 90 pounds of air pressure.

The control valve (not "triple valve"—those went away with K-type brakes in the steam era) on each car is connected to the train line. It performs several functions mechanically based on sensing pressure changes in the train line.

Connected to the control valve is the air reservoir, which stores the car's air supply for braking. The reservoir has two halves: auxiliary or service (normal) and emergency. As the train line is charging, the control valve directs air to the reservoir, charging it to the same pressure as the train line.

To apply the brakes, the engineer opens the brake valve in the locomotive. This allows air (measured in pounds) to escape from the train line. The control valve on each car senses the drop in pressure and directs a corresponding percentage of air from

7

The B end of a covered hopper illustrates typical placement of brake gear and other appliances. *Trains magazine collection*

the service portion of the car's reservoir to the brake cylinder.

Air entering the brake cylinder moves the piston out from the end of the cylinder. The piston movement, via levers, pulls rods attached to the brake beams on each truck. This motion pushes the brake shoes against the wheel treads, applying the brakes. The more braking needed, the more air is released from the train line.

To release the brakes, the engineer closes the valve and compressors begin charging the train line. When the control valves sense the increase in pressure, they release the brakes, and begin recharging the brake reservoirs.

To make an emergency application, all of the air is released from the train line (known as "big-holing" the brakes). All the air from each car's reservoir, including the emergency portion, moves from the reservoir to the cylinder.

A power hand brake, consisting of a brake wheel (or lever) mounted on a gearbox, is located on one end of each car (or on the side of the car at the end), **7**. From the gearbox, a vertical rod and lever connect to the end of the piston on the brake cylinder. Turning the wheel pulls out the piston, applying the brakes. The brake wheel is used both as a parking brake for cars, and by crew members riding cars to position and stop them.

The end of the car that has the brake wheel is the "B" end; the opposite end is the "A" end.

Power hand brakes have been

made by several companies, including Peacock, Universal, Miner, Superior, and Ajax. At one time each manufacturer had a unique brake wheel design, but by the 1960s a standard design had been adopted by all manufacturers.

Brake wheels were mounted at the top of car ends until 1966, when the requirement for running boards was eliminated. Brake wheels are now mounted lower on the car end.

The retaining valve is used at times when descending steep or long grades. Setting the valve keeps a certain amount of air in the brake cylinder while allowing the reservoir to recharge.

Other safety equipment

Running boards (often incorrectly called "roofwalks") were mandatory on new cars until 1966, and shortly after railroads were directed to remove them from existing cars. This was initially to be done by 1974, but the requirement date was eventually pushed to 1983.

Some cars—namely covered hoppers, some tank cars, and coil steel cars—retain them for worker access to loading hatches and fittings. Also, each car must have a platform under the brake wheel.

Ladders and/or grab irons are required at specific locations on each car end and the end of each side. A stirrup step is located at each corner of the car under the ladder or grab irons. These come in many different styles, and can be a spotting feature.

Couplers

Automatic couplers have a moveable knuckle, which opens outward. To couple cars, the knuckle on one or both couplers is opened. One car is backed into the other, and the force causes the knuckles to close and lock automatically. To uncouple cars, a crew member pulls the uncoupling lever, which opens the knuckle on that car and releases the couplers.

Design improvements and variations are signified by letters, with the current Type E and F couplers introduced in the 1930s and 1940s. The type E is the standard coupler; the F is based on the type H tightlock coupler used for passenger service, with a design that eliminates most slack space between couplers (and thus minimizes slack action).

Tank cars carrying hazardous materials were first required to be equipped with shelf-type interlocking couplers in 1970, **8**. Shelf-style couplers help prevent separation in derailments, minimizing the chance that a coupler from an adjoining car will puncture the end of a neighboring tank in an accident.

This expanded to top/bottom shelf couplers required on all new tank cars in 1975, with most older tank cars required to have shelf couplers added by 1979.

Many hopper and coal gondola cars were equipped with rotary couplers starting in the early 1960s. These rotate within their draft-gear boxes, allowing the coupler to turn while still coupled to the adjoining cars, **9**.

An uncoupling lever on each car end extends to the left as you're looking at the car end. Levers (not "lift bars") are made in a variety of styles depending upon the type of coupler and whether the car has extended draft gear because of a cushioning device.

The coupler type and style is often indicated in stenciling on the car end.

Car cushioning

Damage to lading caused by hard coupling and slack action (running in and out while a train is in motion) has long been a concern for railroads. Cushioning systems first appeared

8

Double shelf-style couplers keep couplers aligned and coupled in the event of a derailment. They're required on tank cars and other cars carrying hazardous materials. *Jeff Wilson*

Rotary Coupler

Retainer/wear plate assembly

Ball end of shank rotates inside of housing

Tightlock F-style coupler with added lower shelf

9

Rotary couplers have shanks that can turn in the draft-gear box, allowing cars to be rotated for dumping while still coupled. *Trains magazine illustration*

in the 1920s but were upgraded and became more popular in the 1950s.

Freight-car cushioning systems fall into two types: end-of-car (EOC; also EOCC for end of car cushioning) or center-of-car (COC) units.

The first modern hydraulic COC unit was the Hydra-Cushion in 1955, **10**. It uses a sliding center sill with friction plates and a hydraulic chamber in the middle to cushion slack action, with large springs that return the sill to a normal position. It uses a vertical hydraulic cylinder, which can often be seen below the sill under the middle of the car.

Other COC systems followed, including Keystone (Shock Control), ACF Freight-Saver, and Pullman-Standard Hydroframe. These systems used horizontal hydraulic units that weren't visible from the side. A 20" travel distance was typical for these systems.

Early EOC cushioning was usually some form of rubber-pad draft gear. Hydraulic EOCs began appearing in the 1950s, and gained popularity rapidly, especially on long cars where a moving center sill wasn't practical. The drawing in **11** shows how one Keystone unit works.

These have a hydraulic unit that has a piston behind the coupler with a spring that returns the unit to position. They are made in many variations and varying return distances; 10" and 15" are the most popular.

Today, cars with EOC systems far outnumber COC systems (about 255,000 to 38,000). The popularity of EOC systems increased dramatically as technology improved through the 1970s and later: EOC devices are lighter, less expensive, and easier to install than COC units.

Car lettering often touts the presence of cushioning, sometimes with generic "Cushion Car" lettering but often with specific system references—see Chapter 4 for several examples. The presence of cushioning is also usually obvious in the coupler box, which extends out from the car end to allow travel, **12**.

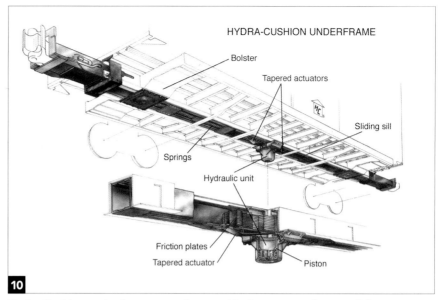

10 Hydra-Cushion and other center-of-car cushioning systems have a sliding center sill with a central hydraulic unit to absorb shock action. *Evans Products*

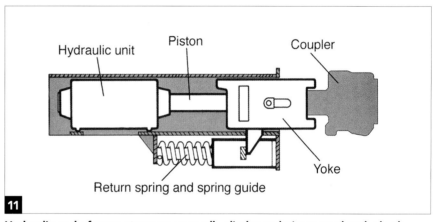

11 Hydraulic end-of-car systems use a small cylinder and piston to absorb shock, with a bottom- or side-mounted spring to return the coupler to normal position. *Keystone*

12 The extended coupler box is a telltale sign of car cushioning. The end-of-car lettering above the coupler advises that the car is equipped with a Keystone Shock Control unit. *Linn Westcott*

Bibliography

Books

American Car & Foundry Box Cars, 1960-1981, by Edward S. Kaminski. Signature Press, 2015

American Car & Foundry Company 1899-1999, by Edward S. Kaminski. Signature Press, 1999

Box Car Production 1963-1994, by David G. Casdorph. Society of Freight Car Historians, 1995

A Catalog of Modern Plastics Cars (Transport History Monograph No. 6), by David G. Casdorph. Society of Freight Car Historians, 1994

Freight Cars of the '40s and '50s, by Jeff Wilson. Kalmbach Media, 2015

Grain Cars 1995/96 (Freight Cars Journal Monograph No. 28), by David G. Casdorph. Society of Freight Car Historians, 1995

The Model Railroader's Guide to Freight Cars, by Jeff Wilson. Kalmbach Media, 2005)

Pressurized Covered Hoppers (Freight Cars Journal Monograph No. 26), by David G. Casdorph. Society of Freight Car Historians, 1995

Tank Car Color Guide, Volume 2: Stub Sill Cars, by James Kinkaid. Morning Sun Books, 2011

Woodchip Cars (Freight Cars Journal Monograph No. 30), by David G. Casdorph. Society of Freight Car Historians, 1995

Periodicals

"4,740-Cubic-Foot-Capacity Covered Hopper Cars," by Jim Eager, *RailModel Journal*, January 1991, p. 55-63

"ACF CF4650 Three-Bay Center Flow Covered Hoppers," by James Eager, *RailModel Journal*, October 1994, p. 23-27

"ACF 17,360-Gallon Chlorine Tank Cars," by Edward S. Kaminski, *RailModel Journal*, December 2001, p. 23-27

"ACF's Precision Design Auto Cars," Parts 1 and 2, by James Kinkaid, *Mainline Modeler*, March 1998, p. 43-48; April 1998, p. 38-44

"Air Brakes for Model Railroaders," by Fred Carlson, *Model Railroader*, November 1994, p. 100-105

"Airslide—Late Production," by Bill McKean, *Mainline Modeler*, January 1987, p. 64-67

"All-Door Boxcar Modeling Options," by Ron Sleeter, *Mainline Modeler*, October 1991, p. 68-71

"Athearn HO Scale PS 5344 Boxcar," Parts 1, 2, and 3, by David G. Casdorph, *Model Railroading*, November 2003, p. 44-49; December 2003, p. 28-33; March 2004, p. 32-35

"Canadian Cylindrical Hoppers, National Steel Car 3,800-cf Cars," by Eric Neubauer, *Railmodel Journal*, November 1991, p. 24-25

"Canadian Pacific Ry. 3,800-Cubic-Foot Hopper," by Patrick Lawson, *Mainline Modeler*, February 1997, p. 72-73

"Canadian Wheat Board Covered Hoppers," *Mainline Modeler*, December 2002, p. 70-72

"Center Beam Flat Cars," by D. Scott Chatfield, *RailModel Journal*, January 1996, p. 29-34

"Center Flow Covered Hoppers," by Mike Del Vecchio and Edward S. Kaminski, *Trains*, February 2000, p. 42-47

"Coil Cars," by James Kinkaid, *Mainline Modeler*, October 1996, p. 42-48

"Consolidated Stencils," by Ed Crist and Jim Panza, *Railroad Model Craftsman*, December 1978, p. 62-65; "Consolidated Stencil Changes," January 1982, p. 77

"Contemporary National Steel Car Covered Hopper Designs," by David G. Casdorph, *Model Railroading*, December 2001, p. 44-47

"Corn Syrup Tank Cars," Parts 1-6, by Tim Frederick, *Model Railroading*, July 2004, p. 26-29; August 2004, p. 44-46; September 2004, p. 40-43; October 2004, p. 42-47; November 2004, p. 42-45; December 2004, p. 32-35

"Covered Hopper" [Evans 4780], by James Kinkaid, *Mainline Modeler*, May 1998, p. 39-45

"Cryogenic Cars," by Thornton Waite, *Mainline Modeler*, August 2000, p. 26-29

"Early Pullman 60-foot Auto Parts Cars," by James Kinkaid, *Mainline Modeler*, February 1998, p. 40-47

"The Evans Gondola," by James Kinkaid, *Mainline Modeler*, February 1999, p. 28-32

"FMC Covered Hopper," by Jeffrey M. Koeller, *Mainline Modeler*, May 1992, p. 31-33

"Freight Car Cushioning Devices," *Southern & Southwestern Railway Club Proceedings, Volume 41, No. 9*, January 1966

"From Composite to Coalporter," by Tom Hoff, *Mainline Modeler*, December 1995, p. 32-40

"GATX Arcticar," by Mark W. Heinz, *Mainline Modeler*, September 1992, p. 25-29

"Identifying FMC/Gunderson Boxcars 1972-1997," by David Casdorph, *Mainline Modeler*, January 1998, p. 26-31

"IPD, Railbox, and Other Cars from the Boxcar Boom of the 1970s," by Jim Eager, *RailModel Journal*, March 2002, p. 40-47; May 2002, p. 40-43; June 2002, p. 36-40; September 2002, p. 24-29; October 2002, p. 40-45, November 2002, p. 41-47

"Johnstown America's Grainporter," by David S. Lehlbach, *Railroad Model*

Craftsman, September 2003, p. 66

"KCS Covered Hopper" [Thrall 4750], by Jim Fite and Mark Hills, *Mainline Modeler*, April 1990, p. 26-29

"Making the Connection," by Richard Dawson, *Trains*, August 2000, p. 55-62

"Modeler's Guide to Freight Car Trucks," by Jeff Wilson, *Model Railroader*, December 2003, p. 72-77

"Modern 50-foot PS-1," Parts 1 and 2, by James Kinkaid, *Mainline Modeler*, April 1994, p. 39-44; May 1994, p. 28-33

"Modern Tank Cars," Parts 1 and 2, by John J. Ryczkowski, *Mainline Modeler*, February 1992, p. 58-62; May 1992, p. 71-75

"Modern Tank Cars: Acid-Type Cars," by John J. Ryczkowski, *Mainline Modeler*, September 1992, p. 45-49

"National Steel Car Plastic Pellet Hoppers," by D. Scott Chatfield, *RailModel Journal*, December 2001, p. 12-15

"PFE's Mechanical Reefers," by Tony Thompson, *Railroad Model Craftsman*, January 1988, p. 76-85

"PS-2 Covered Hoppers," Parts 1, 2, and 3, by Martin Lofton, *Mainline Modeler*, July 1991, p. 68-73; August 1991, p. 69-73; November 1991, p. 66-70

"Pressure Tank Cars," by John Ryczkowski, *Mainline Modeler*, November 1992, p. 46-51

"Pullman-Standard 3,000-cf Covered Hopper," by Robert L. Hundman, *Mainline Modeler*, May 1984, p. 80-82

"Pullman-Standard 4427 PS-2CD Covered Hopper" [low-side car], by James Kinkaid, *Mainline Modeler*,

"Pullman-Standard 4427 PS-2CD High-Side Covered Hopper," Parts 1 and 2, by James Kinkaid, *Mainline Modeler*, March 1995, p. 64-69; April 1995, p. 28-31

"Pullman-Standard PS-3 Hoppers," by James Kinkaid, *Mainline Modeler*, June 1995, p. 26-30

"Pullman-Standard: Pullman Leasing," by David Casdorph, *Mainline Modeler*, April 1989, p. 24-29

"Roller-Bearing Trucks, Part 1: Prototype," by John Ryczkowski, *Mainline Modeler*, September 1993, p. 50-55

"SAL/CB&Q Cement Hopper," by Robert L. Hundman, *Mainline Modeler*, November 1989, p. 54-55

"The Smart Money Rides on Boxcars," by Paul J. Dolkos, *Trains*, September 1978, p. 22-26

"Southern Coal Gondola: The 'Silversides' Car," by James Kinkaid, *Mainline Modeler*, April 2004, p. 36-42

"Southern Waffle Boxcar: 50-foot Pullman-Standard," by Robert L. Hundman, *Mainline Modeler*, August 1990, p. 24-27

"Tank car Qualification Stencils," by Stuart Streit, *Railroad Model Craftsman*, September 2002, p. 83-86

"Tank Cars," by David G. Casdorph, *Model Railroading*, February 1995, p. 50-53

"Thrall's 52' Gondola Cars Since 1963," Parts 1 and 2, by David G. Casdorph, *Model Railroading*, May 1996, p. 6-9; June 1996, p. 25-27

"Trinity 5161," Parts 1-6, by David G. Casdorph, *Model Railroading*, March 2003, p. 42-45; April 2003, p. 44-47; May 2003, p. 44-47, June 2003, p. 46-49; July 2003, p. 46-49; August 2003, p. 46-49

"TTX Company's FBOX," by David G. Casdorph, *Model Railroading*, June 2005, p. 46-49

"TTX Company's TBOX," by David G. Casdorph, *Model Railroading*, July 2005, p. 44-47

"2,600-cf Airslide Covered Hopper Cars (1953-1959)," Parts 1 and 2, by Ed Hawkins, *Railroad Prototype Cyclopedia*

"Walthers HO & N Scale 76-Foot Cryogenic Reefers," by Scott Chatfield, *RailModel Journal*, March 1994, p. 4-7

Miscellaneous
AAR Circular No. OT-10, Code of Car Service Rules (Association of American Railroads, 2018)

AAR Guide for Railroads (Association of American Railroads/Railinc, 2018)

Ensuring Railroad Tank Car Safety (Transportation Research Board, National Research Council, 1994)

Field Guide to Tank Cars, Third Edition (Association of American Railroads Transportation Technology Center, 2017)

Improving Freight Train Operation with ABD Valves (Westinghouse Air Brake Division)

"Maximizing Safety and Weight: A White Paper on 263K+ Tank Cars," by James H. Rader, Federal Railroad Administration, and Jean-Pierre Gagnon, Transport Canada

The North American Freight Railcar Review, 2018 (Railinc/AAR, 2018)

Railroad Freight Car Safety Standards (Federal Railroad Administration; various editions)

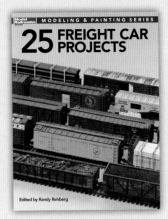

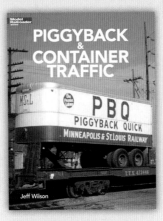
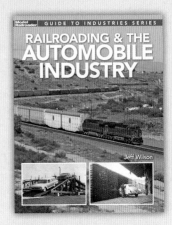